Law, Politics and the Gender Binary

The distinction between male and female, or masculinity and femininity, has long been considered to be foundational to society and the organization of its institutions. In the last decades, the massive literature on gender has challenged this discursive construction. Gender has been disassembled and reassembled, variously considered as social practice, performance, ideology. Yet the binary relationship 'man/woman' continues to be a characteristic trait of Western societies. This book gathers together contributions by experts in various fields – including law, sociology, philosophy and anthropology – to pin down the relationship between institutions and the gender binary. Centrally, it examines the way in which the present-day gender binary is shored up by the conceptualization and regulation of sex and gender at societal and institutional levels. Based on this examination, it tackles the issue of what the practices and processes of subjectivation are that preserve this binary distinction as the foundation of gender. Each of the chapters discusses this pressing question with a view to considering whether current equality policies challenge hierarchical and hegemonic understandings of gender or are the residue of a sexist understanding of gender. This analysis then paves the way for a more general and crucial question: whether institutions can, or should, contribute to the process of deconstructing the gender binary.

Petr Agha is the director of the Centre for Law and Public Affairs, a researcher at the Institute of State and Law, Czech Academy of Sciences, and a senior lecturer at the Faculty of Law of Charles University in Prague.

Law, Politics and the Gender Binary

Edited by Petr Agha

Routledge
Taylor & Francis Group
a GlassHouse Book

First published 2019
by Routledge
2 Park Square, Milton Park, Abingdon, Oxon OX14 4RN

and by Routledge
52 Vanderbilt Avenue, New York, NY 10017

First issued in paperback 2020

Routledge is an imprint of the Taylor & Francis Group, an informa business

A GlassHouse book

British Library Cataloguing-in-Publication Data
A catalogue record for this book is available from the British Library

Library of Congress Cataloging-in-Publication Data
Names: Agha, Petr, editor.
Title: Law, politics and the gender binary / edited by Petr Agha. Description:
Abingdon, Oxon ; New York, NY : Routledge, 2019. | Includes
    bibliographical references and index.
Identifiers: LCCN 2018022497 | ISBN 9781138486058 (hbk)
Subjects: LCSH: Sexual minorities—Legal status, laws, etc. | Gender
    identity—Law and legislation.
Classification: LCC K3242.3 .L39 2019 | DDC 342.08/5—dc23
LC record available at https://lccn.loc.gov/2018022497

ISBN 13: 978-0-367-67045-0 (pbk)
ISBN 13: 978-1-138-48605-8 (hbk)

Typeset in Times New Roman
by Swales & Willis Ltd, Exeter, Devon, UK

Contents

Acknowledgements

This book, *Law, Politics and the Gender Binary*, as well as Chapter 5, 'Subjectivity, gender and agency', has received financial support from the research project 'Transsexuality and the problem of minority identity in legal discourse' (GACR 14-35646S) awarded to the Institute of State and Law of the Academy of Sciences of the Czech Republic, created under subsidies for a long-term conceptual development (RVO: 68378122).

Antu Sorainen would like to acknowledge the financial support of the research projects 'Wills and inheritance in sexually marginalised groups: a multidisciplinary study' (funded by the Academy of Finland, grant number 277203) and 'CoreKin: contrasting and re-imagining margins of kinship' (funded by the Academy of Finland, grant number 297957) for Chapter 6, 'How the inheritance system thinks: queering kinship, gender and care in the legal sphere'.

Contributors

Petr Agha is the director of the Centre for Law and Public Affairs, a researcher at the Institute of State and Law, Czech Academy of Sciences, and a senior lecturer at the Faculty of Law of Charles University in Prague.

Francesca Romana Ammaturo is a lecturer in sociology and human rights at the University of Roehampton, UK. Her research focuses on the rights of lesbian, gay, bisexual, trans and intersex people in Europe.

Carlotta Cossutta is a research fellow in political philosophy at the University of Eastern Piedmont. Her research interests are primarily critical theory and feminist and queer thinking.

Ingrid Salvatore is University Researcher in Political Philosophy at the University of Salerno. She teaches Gender Studies at Luiss University (Rome).

Antu Sorainen is a fellow of the Academy of Finland and a docent in gender studies, working at the University of Helsinki. She has conducted empirical studies in the area of queer sexualities in the legal field. She is the co-author of a book on the conceptual history of *Sittlichkeit* and has published recently on queer inheritance practices. Sorainen is the principal investigator of the research project 'Wills and inheritance practices in sexually marginalised groups" (Academy of Finland, 2014–19) and the director of the research team "CoreKin: contrasting and re-imagining margins of kinship" (Academy of Finland, 2016–20).

Valeria Venditti received a PhD in political philosophy from Sapienza University of Rome. Her interests include feminist theory, queer theory and socio-legal studies. She is currently working on legal inclusion and alternative forms of the legitimation of non-traditional ways of living and identities, relationships and kinship ties.

Introduction

The main objective of this book is to tackle the tricky questions of whether dismantling the gender binary is desirable, possible or beneficial and, more fundamentally, whether institutions could or should contribute to this undertaking. In doing so, the contributors aim to analyse the relationship between politico-juridical institutions (their language, products and organizational patterns) and the functioning of gender as a conceptual and pragmatic device at both social and institutional levels. Therefore, the core questions it addresses concern the relationship between the way in which institutions operate and the interplay between law, institutions and the social realm. Do institutions have to register and mirror the way in which social actors think of and organize their relationships to each other? Or should they seek to foreground and redress the potentially dysfunctional, biased and unfair outcomes of this pre-/extra-institutional organization? And how, and to what extent, do institutions affect or even produce – rather than merely register and mirror – the conceptual and pragmatic lines whereby social actors think of and organize their relationships to each other? To put it bluntly, should institutions try to foster gender equality by remedying resilient social constructs as well as their distinctions and disparities? Or, by doing so, are institutions unwittingly contributing to their persistence? If so, should institutions go faster than society and just drop the gender binary by striking it from all texts, documents, reports, and so on? Would an institutional 'silencing' of the gender binary help to dismantle the detrimental outcomes that it is claimed to engender? Or would this end up being a way of pretending that the gender binary does not exist and so failing to govern its dynamics?

These crucial questions are tackled by interrogating and problematizing recent societal, political and legal evolutions that are generally designed to address the gender binary. The distinction between male and female, or masculinity and femininity, has long been considered to be foundational to society and the organization of its institutions. In the last decades, the massive literature on gender has challenged many pillars of this discursive construction as feeding off deep-rooted, but prejudiced, understandings of human nature and human sociality. Gender has been disassembled and reassembled, variously considered as social practice, performance, ideology. Yet the binary relationship 'man/woman' continues to be regarded as a characterizing trait of Western societies (even in those sexual equality agendas that, whether inadvertently or not, reinstate a lexicon of difference). Whether it is a reification that is insensitive to historicization or a genuinely natural trait of the human, gender is one of the pivots of social organization. As a consequence, the hierarchies, power differentials and sexist biases overtly and covertly attached to it continue to permeate the social world and to affect social actors' principles of vision and division.

In the present political environment, this topic encompasses a variety of disparate and passionate debates over the form and substance of public policy, given the fact that traditional binaries have historically been the basis for exclusionary, if not discriminatory, public policy. One of the key questions that touches upon the most fundamental legal evolutions pertaining to the gender binary is that of the politicization of sexuality. In light of the modern historical struggle against identity-based binaries that began in the 1960s, and recent resistance and protests centred on racial, ethnic, sex/gender and socio-economic critiques of societal order, traditional binary-based identities require re-examination. In particular, it is necessary to re-evaluate the underlying assumptions and effects of a binary-based cultural and social identity matrix, as well as what place, if any, binary-based signifiers have in the present. In light of the role that politicized identity is playing in the present, and the national political and legal debates that have been triggered by various groups challenging the integrity of identity-based binaries, **Ingrid Salvatore** examines the fundamental conflict between the move toward re-establishing identity-based binaries (and their underlying assumptions) and resistance to such binaries. In her contribution, Salvatore goes beyond the traditionally accepted understanding of what the politicization of sexuality entails and moves away from the traditional habitus of feminism by investigating the constitution of sexual identity as a trait traditionally considered one of the most basic forms of personal identity. Politicizing the domestic role of women was the first aim of feminism. Ingrid explores two dominant strands of feminism, liberal and radical, to show how each perceived the functional structure of society. She concludes that feminism has primarily been a fight for the politicization of sexuality and against a paradigmatic identity.

The conflict between those adhering to traditional binaries and those questioning the assumptions underlying those binaries can be readily observed in law and public policy. Indeed, law plays a central role in these questions, with many of the actions taken and policies advanced being challenged in the courts. Legal challenges to identity-based binaries have exposed a complex relationship between the courts' reliance on binary-based constructs to administer justice and their combating of discriminatory policies and practices. Ironically, the courts have relied on legal schema that utilize such signifiers to protect vulnerable and marginalized communities. Human rights law, and rights talk in general, has been one of the principal avenues in which issues of gender identity have been addressed. **Francesca Romana Ammaturo** considers the opportunities and limitations that gendered conceptions of human rights represent in the context of the Council of Europe. Her chapter asks whether human rights and the gender binary should be radically decoupled to accommodate people whose gender identity and/or sexual orientation question or transcend the 'male/female' dichotomy, as well as whether abandoning the gender binary in the field of human rights is feasible and/or desirable. She discusses how creative practices of 'multisexual citizenship', whereby individuals selectively appropriate or deploy specific sexed or gendered identitarian configurations in their daily life, may radically challenge the highly gendered concept of the 'human rights subject'. She shows how the relationship between gender and institutions has been problematic since their beginning, institutions themselves having been the first to have contributed, often decisively, to the production and reproduction of sexism. In this chapter, having re-examined the integrity of the binary, Ammaturo lays out critical reflection and debate, and provides the framework within which to discuss the politics and complexity of identity within the law that contextualizes binary.

The law cultivates historically based identity binaries when converting sociocultural and economic realities into legal discourse. The law and the courts, generally speaking, are based on whether a subject fits or does not fit into a legal identity signifier. Subjects find themselves emplaced within binary identities; an identity is manufactured and given to subjects by various political, economic, social or legal elites. Yet the law views actuality in terms of categories, classifications, identity-based signifiers. To deconstruct binaries without discarding them – that is, to identify and explicitly acknowledge the deep effect that the binary has, and the serious distortions and limitations that are immanent within it – we can begin a process of productively 'destabilizing' binaries. In so doing, these binaries can be recognized as dynamic, rather than static, and as fundamentally contingent, rather than universal.

To investigate the essence of legal binarism, one needs to start from an analysis of those legal norms that somehow challenge the traditional positioning of gendered bodies into society through the implementation of inclusive policies. **Carlotta Cossutta** examines the relationship between politicized identity, culture and the binary-based nature of identity in the law, and identifies two particular dynamics that shaped the behaviour of institutions: the discrimination of some groups – from women to gay, trans and intersex people, etc.; and the use of a neutral universal to act in the opposite direction, rendering the same groups invisible. In so doing, she intends to emphasize the importance of revisiting the binary as it is conceptualized and applied in law, and hence it is necessary to define some of the key terms employed in the remainder of this work. The basic unit of analysis vis-à-vis the binary is that of the 'juridical subject' as a doctrinal entity. Such a subject has rights and obligations under law, and may qualify for judicial protections if the courts find that the subject falls within a specified legal classification. Legal identity thus comprises the space within which the subject and the law interact; it is an identity that is conferred upon the subject by law that entitles a subject to claim the protections of identity-based legislation. However a 'non-binary identity' is one in which the subject is not encased within a clear biaxial 'This/That' classification, category or structure. A subject is therefore not immured in a racial, ethnic, sex, gender or other identity category that is fundamentally binary-based. Cossutta explores these dynamics with a view to answering the question of what the role of institutions could be in the subversion of gender binarism, focusing primarily on the language of institutions.

Law, in the form of judicial interpretation, has been employed to recognize and confer legal status, protections and benefits upon those who fall within certain identity-based group classifications. Many aspects of a subject's social and legal reality – rights, freedoms, responsibilities, duties and obligations – are directly impacted when courts interpret identity-based legislation, broadly construed. Race, ethnicity and sexuality are exemplars of identity-based signifiers that manifest in the law. In response to this, **Valeria Venditti** tackles the question of gender binarism in the law by considering 'gender-sensitive' regulation. She demonstrates that (and how) inclusive legal measures modify the social relations they target by redesigning them according to a language that was, until that point, alien to that very relation. She achieves this through the analysis of different instances that characterize the way in which marginalized social groups negotiate the terms of their inclusion. Venditti concludes that, since inclusive policies are essentially linked with binarism and naturally reinforce it, legal inclusion is bounded to dislocate marginalization. Even though the dynamics analysed so far are continually in flux, be it the symbolic order or individual performances of identity, or the law, it appears that the constraints of binary possibilities within the realm of the law represent a forceful imposition on the multitude of ways in which the communicative action that forms the contents and contours of the discursive possibilities transpires. The interplay between gender performance and its reception, understanding and interpretation against the backdrop of the law is another important aspect that needs to be examined when talking about the role of law and institutions and the gender binary.

Identities once considered viable and concrete in the recent past, such as sexuality, gender, race and ethnicity, seem to be quite fluid, and perhaps not amenable to the present sociocultural and political actuality, as we head into the mid-21st century. Yet it seems that identities in the present have also become more complex, fragmented, disparate and expansively inclusive – to the point at which the idea of identity may have become overly porous, easily breached or so nuanced with sub-identities that the initial basic binary loses its integrity and coherency, and fails to provide clear criteria for defining any discernible identity. The parallel contexts, legal and social, exist alongside each other, continuously influencing and acting upon each other. As a result, some sub-identities that have not been integrated are subjugated and exist on the periphery of the binary, while others are essentially silenced because they cannot be expressed in the dominant context. The binary nature of identity, which includes the political and the legal, establishes what Michel Foucault has termed 'grids of specification', which he defines as 'the systems according to which the different "kinds of [knowledge]" are divided, contrasted, related, regrouped, classified, derived from one another as objects of . . . discourse'.[1] Identity emerges within these grids, which we conceive of as binaries. The binary nature of the legal subject limits how one can define one's self in lived social experience. These binaries delineate and make 'real' the abstract space in which the law processes identity-based cases and controversies. The essential 'trade-off' between the efficiency of the binary and its inclusive nature is that the law, in its limited perception of juridical subjects in binary terms, cannot give a voice to subjects that exist, socially, outside a traditional binary structure. The historical or traditional binary creates a point on which signifiers can be employed to settle legal cases and controversies that involve basing decision-making processes on simplified signifiers. The binary thus has been, and continues to be, the site at which the courts construct legal identity.

The model – the binary – manufactures truth-value, but it is also subject, like all models and constructs, to revision and reconfiguration. The contradictory nature of identity, in the locus of a subject that shapes the world and is shaped by it, may clear a space for accountability in the culturally relativist landscape contoured by law and policy. The historical modernist binary that the law has employed is based upon a classificatory schema that builds legal actuality from relations of power. How we see bodies is an effect of the discursive field within which we are located. Particular regimes of power

---

1 M. Foucault, *The Archaeology of Knowledge* (New York: Harper Colophon, 1972), p. 48.

inform the discursive fields that define and shape both the materiality and meaning of bodies. Discursive fields are themselves made up of competing discourses that produce different subject positions and forms of identity. Subjectivity (consisting of an individual's conscious and unconscious sense of self, emotions and desires) is also constituted in language and rational consciousness is only one dimension of subjectivity. It is in the process of using language – whether as thought or speech – that we take up positions as speaking and thinking subjects and the identities that go with them.

In his chapter, **Petr Agha** explores the relationship between the form and the substance of 'doing the law' by conceptualizing the relationship between individual performance and the performativity of the law. Unlike individual performance, performativity is not unique to a specific person; rather, it pre-supposes the existence of a symbolic order in which the social and political context, including gender performances, is represented. Agha analyses the stories of trans people in the Czech Republic, and explores how their bod-ies create and shape relationships with others, as well as how their bodies confirm their (own gender) identities against the backdrop of the symbolic order in place, visibly represented by the law and medical discourse. To do so, he uses data acquired during semi-structured interviews conducted in the Czech Republic, with an eye to analysing how transgender individuals shape their (own) social identities in the interplay between the law, society and medical discourse. For these reasons, it is important to explore how alternative kinship, non-normative sexualities and gender cut through the gender binary, as well as the relationship between politico-juridical institu-tions and the functioning of gender as a conceptual and pragmatic device at both social and institutional levels.

The persistence of the binary, despite calls to blur or discard the identity signifiers that create an enclosed and identifiable identity space, is illustra-tive of the complex processes that are at work in the evolution of thought pertaining to identity and the configuration of politics and the law. **Antu Sorainen** draws on queer and feminist anthropologist literature on institu-tions, legal categories and relationships, and points out the vulnerability risks that gender produces in relation to the growing importance of the inheritance institution – in particular, the potentially problematic engage-ments with this institution by those who find themselves in the sexually marginalized groups or on the margins of kinship. A study of a declining Nordic welfare state provides a concrete foundation on which to open up wider questions on how gender, queer sexuality and kinship interact with legal institutions. The discussion is based on original survey and interview research data on queer inheritance arrangements and lawyers' experiments with their queer clients. It analyses how gender distinctions and sexual valorisations get mobilized in and through the inheritance system.

This collective book therefore gathers contributions by experts in various fields (law, sociology, philosophy and anthropology) to pin down the relationship between institutions and the gender binary. It first explores the conceptual lines that shore up the present-day gender binary in the face of far-reaching transformations in the conceptualization and regulation of sex and gender at societal and institutional levels. Based on this, it tackles the issue of what the practices and processes of subjectivation are that preserve the binary distinction as the foundation of gender. The various contributors discuss these pressing questions with a view to understanding whether, and to what extent, equality policies challenge hierarchical and hegemonic understandings of gender, or are simply the residue of a sexist understanding of gender. This analysis paves the way towards a more general and crucial question: whether, and to what extent, institutions can, could or should contribute to the multifarious process of deconstructing the gender binary.

1   The politicisation of sexuality
Feminism, difference, differences

Ingrid Salvatore

If anything qualifies politics as a field of research, it is its controversial relationship with naturalism. Because nature is governed by laws independent of us, all that falls under its domain is unamendable. A naturalistic view of the social order seems, *eo ipso*, to legitimate a given status quo. Political authority, slavery, poverty and racism have often been justified or explained on natural bases. It is no surprise, then, that emancipatory movements have been generally suspicious of 'naturalism' and have seen nature as inadequate for grounding politics. But this is not all that I mean by 'politicisation'. What distinguishes politicisation as a theoretical enterprise is that it aims not only to reject a given argument as false or ungrounded, but also to explain the role it plays in structuring or legitimating a subsisting social arrangement. Many movements have dealt with politicisation and unravelled the political character of purported natural arguments. Sexuality is one among these.

This chapter offers a reconstruction of the politicisation of sexuality, starting with where it all began: the feminist movement. I will try to show how women battled to gain a denaturalised, *political* status and how the very conception of this fight changed over time. Women are certainly not the only group interested in the politicisation of sexuality. I take feminism as an obvious point of departure, however, not only because feminism was the first movement in which the politicisation of sexuality was formulated, but also because the main interest of this chapter is to sketch out how feminism has impacted sexuality in general. Whilst feminists throughout all of history have had a political conception of the sexual identification of women, I will show how the rejection of naturalism might not be enough to achieve a sexually unbiased society. As feminism has changed its conception of the political nature of women's sexual identification, so too have feminism's normative implications changed. The possibility exists that feminism may now play a more regressive, than progressive, role in changing the social view of sexuality and sex classifications. The chapter will conclude by briefly considering what, if anything, we can understand regarding the relationship between politics and naturalism.

Feminism, nonetheless, first requires a few words.

As Alison Jaggar (1983, p. 3) has written, it may be true that 'feminism has always existed'. However, I consider feminism not only *the fact* of women's oppression, but also the systematic reflection of women on the causes of their social condition. So viewed, feminism was born in the heart of the Enlightenment, the ideals of which deeply permeated women's reflections and thoughts, and gave rise to feminism as a distinct phenomenon.[1]

When the Enlightenment's ideals first appeared, the few women who got the chance to participate actively, often at the cost of their personal reputations, did not conceive of themselves as feminists. Convinced as they were that the Enlightenment was a battle of men, as well as of women, they thought that the social change they were all fighting for was the general improvement of men's and women's lives.

As the Enlightenment removed old customs and habits as sources of legitimacy and promoted principles of equal freedom for all, what more could women desire? Rights granted by the state would have protected women from the abusive power of husbands, fathers and brothers, by allowing women to lead lives of their own. Enlightenment was their home. Quite soon, however, women discovered that *men* were born equal, not women; that freedom for all meant freedom for all *men*, not for all women and men; that the new society of men was destined to remain the old, familiar one for women.

It is here that feminism began. It began when women started noticing that the very same liberal philosophers who were celebrating the power of man's reason over nature were still depicting women as mere natural beings, too weak for self-governing. This explains why first feminism's writings and polemics were primarily addressed not to conservatives, but to the Enlightenment intellectuals. It is to the authors of the 1789 'Declaration of the Rights of Man and of the Citizen' that Olympe de Gouges addresses her Declaration of the Rights of Woman two years later. And it is Rousseau – the writer whose genius 'I admire' and 'whose opinions I shall often have occasions to cite' – that Mary Wollstonecraft (1996 [1792], p. 24) asks to justify his blindness to the misery of women's lives. But feminists didn't stop at critiques; they engaged in the theoretical work

---

1 A different point of departure for the raising of women's consciousness with respect to the iniquity of their social condition is when, during the Renaissance, they were finally permitted to become educated (Millett 1991 [1977]), p. 65). However, Millett (1991 [1977]), p. 66) also considers the Enlightenment to be a probable birthdate for feminism.

of trying to explain why this was happening. They saw how, if rights were conceded to them, the arrangement of the family would have been altered – but men were fighting to gain new rights and entitlements, not to lose those they had always had![2]

Accordingly, feminism was, first of all, a fight to undo women's natural differences from men – starting with their capacity to give birth – in the political sphere.

From a theoretical point of view, however, it is interesting to note how, in their fight to make women politically equal to men, liberal feminists were among the first to face an important philosophical question that would have a deep impact on both feminism and political philosophy.[3]

According to the classic liberal view, not every form of power relation is oppressive. Whether it is or not depends on its being justified by the practical necessity of protecting the greatest enjoyment of freedom for each. Only institutions that are not so justified are oppressive. Such a conception of oppression describes people as oppressed only insofar as they are not in the condition of exercising a previously assumed liberty. Oppression is the impossibility of enjoying that freedom – an impediment to it.

To see freedom and oppression in this way, however, is to assume, implicitly or explicitly, that people *want* to be free, *believe* themselves to be born equal and *desire* equal treatment. This was not such an easy assumption for feminists. At first, feminists were a tiny minority who did not have women's support.[4] Feminists had to explain why, contrary to their interests, women were rejecting rights and choosing oppression. In facing such a theoretical challenge, feminists modified the classic liberal view of oppression. Feminists had to show that women were unable to *realise* not only the preferences, desires and volition that they had, but also that their very preferences, desires and volition were under men's control. As John Stuart Mill (1995 [1869], p. 132) would observe a few years later, a woman is often 'not a forced slave, but a willing one'; for 'men do not want solely the obedience of women, they want their sentiments', enslaving not only their bodies, but also their minds. If men's oppression might be depicted as the mere impossibility of getting what they (legitimately) want, women did not even dare to want. They

---

2   All through her *Vindication*, Wollstonecraft (1996 [1792]) tries to prove that men have not only nothing to lose from women's rights, but all to gain. Equal rights are actually the only foundation on which the family can be based.

3   With the possible exception of Rousseau.

4   This does not amount to denying that the official historiography has generally ignored women, making their presence even less visible now than it was then: see Phillips (1998). Nonetheless, the very life of Olympe de Gouges, who died alone on the guillotine, proves enough.

were oppressed and did not even know that they were (Wollstonecraft 1996 [1792], p. 52.) This is why feminists insisted so strongly on education.[5] Women's lack of education played a role in feminist thought similar to the role that poverty played in socialism. Uneducated women were the willing allies of their oppressors. Only education could make women fully rational beings.

It must be said that, insofar as liberal feminists were trying to explain why women accepted men's domination, there is a sense in which they were already engaged in politicising sexuality. Nonetheless, it was essentially a sketch of an empirical psychology that they intuited. This sense of politicisation changes profoundly as the feminist reflection progresses.

Despite their unpromising beginnings, the feminists' ideas formed in the Enlightenment gained more and more ground. Though the road was slow and bumpy, women's struggle for their rights advanced up to the time at which two world wars imposed a long period of silence on what would later be called first-wave feminism.

At the end of the Second World War, however, the general impression was that even though it was not as much as many wanted or expected, feminists had accomplished something. It is probably because of this impression that people were shocked when, in *The Feminine Mystique*, Betty Friedan (2010 [1963], p. 6) showed that women's condition in the 1960s was almost as painful as it had always been. In a sociological style, Friedan presented a series of data showing how, despite their recent and in some ways glorious past, women were moving backwards:

> By the end of the nineteen-fifties, the average marriage age of women in America dropped to 20 . . . The proportion of women attending college . . . dropped from 47 percent in 1920 to 35 percent in 1958 [. . .] By the end of the fifties the United States' birthrate was overtaking India's.

Magazines celebrated the movement of American women back to the home: 'A century earlier, women had fought for higher education; now girls went to college to get a husband' (Friedan 2010 [1963], p. 6). The suburban housewife, kissing her husband goodbye, smiling as she ran the new electric waxer, baking her own bread and changing 'the sheets

---

5 Wollstonecraft's *Vindication* is addressed to Talleyrand as the author of a report on education from which women were excluded (Wollstonecraft 1996 [1792], p. 1). All through her book, Wollstonecraft insists on the vital importance of women's education. See also Mill (1995 [1869], p. 132).

on the bed twice a week instead of once', 'was the dream image of the young American' (Friedan 2010 [1963], p. 8). Women had obtained the right to do otherwise, but it looked as though they spent all their emotional investment on becoming the perfect spouse. A new wave of feminism was beginning. But now, the theoretical framework of first-wave feminism, with its roots in liberal individualism, was largely unable to provide a plausible account of what was happening to women (Jaggar 1983).

Betty Friedan's book appeared a few years after the 1949 publication of Simon de Beauvoir's very influential *The Second Sex*,[6] a powerful critique of the abstract individual that became paradigmatic both in Anglo-American and continental feminism. De Beauvoir (1953 [1949], ch. I) agrees with liberal feminists' opposition to the naturalistic view of women. She also agrees that the naturalised woman is largely men's invention. According to de Beauvoir (1953 [1949], p. 16), in our patriarchal socie-ties, women represent the *Other* of men, where the *Other* is the bearer of anything that can restore you from the miseries of your life. The more the *Other* is degraded, the more you are safe. If women are said to be stupid, men can feel clever and smart. If women are said to be weak, men can feel strong and courageous. If women are irrational and sentimental, men can feel rational and self-governing.[7] But de Beauvoir radically departs from liberal feminists on their claim that to be an individual sexually different from another means nothing.

For liberal feminists, as we have seen, women's troubles derive from the premise that, because women can have babies and can help them to survive, men *wrongly infer* that this is women's *essence* and that, because of this essence, women must be excluded from the political sphere. What liberal feminists claimed instead is that sex had to have for women the same political importance that it had for men: none. Such a claim, according to de Beauvoir (1953 [1949], p. 14), is a theoretical mistake, with harmful political consequences: '[It] is stoutly affirmed by those who hold to the philosophy of the enlightenment, of rationalism, of nominalism, [that] the word women [has] no specific content [. . .], that there is no longer any place for woman as such.' But nominalism is 'a rather inadequate doctrine' for de Beauvoir (1953 [1949], p. 14):

---

6 How much influence Friedan had is a matter of controversy among feminists. While Jaggar (1983, p. 37) tends to present her as a liberal thinker, Karen Vintges (1999, p. 134) reports Friedan recognising, only years later, de Beauvoir's influence.
7 See de Beauvoir's analysis of a misogynistic writer such as Montherlant: de Beauvoir (1953 [1949], pp. 212–225).

Surely, woman is, like man, a human being, but . . . [t]he fact is that . . . [t]o decline to accept such notions as the eternal feminine, the black soul, the Jewish character, is not to deny that Jews, Negroes, women exist today – this denial does not represent a liberation for those concerned but rather a flight from reality.

Because any individual can exist only in a determined, embodied, socially situated form, de Beauvoir takes for granted that individuals exist as exactly *those* individuals: ignoring who they are is 'a flight from reality'. If we cannot be individuals apart from being a certain kind of individual, the answer to the male creation of women is not a flight into an abstract individualism, but into women's creation of female.

Second-wave feminism thus turned from a theory of equality among individuals into a theory of difference between men and women. Liberal feminists had thought *of being a woman* as a political impediment from which they had to escape – the sooner, the better – and withdraw into individualism. Second-wave feminism rejected both individualism and naturalism, and adopted instead a very different paradigm. As neither a natural kind nor a collection of individuals, women in feminism came to be conceived as classes are conceived in Marxism (de Beauvoir 1953 [1949], pp. 17*ff*).[8] Like a class, 'woman' is a socially constituted object. But, unlike a class, women's existence depends on patriarchy. From a Marxist perspective, however, the existence of social objects strictly depends on *economy*. This is what a social class consists of. Any social object that cannot be explained on an economic basis cannot be said to exist. Insofar as the existence of women as a social object does not rest on an economic basis, women, like men, can be *natural* objects, similar to birds or trees. But they cannot exist as a social entity. Feminists have attempted to explain women as a social category within a strictly Marxian framework, but their explanations have generally remained trapped in materialism – that is, the socialist question eclipses the feminist question, which again amounts to denying that women exist as a social object (Engels 2010 [1884]; Farrelly 2011; Haines 1997). Feminists had to provide a theory of patriarchy.

Women must exist as a socially constituted object *unexplained by economy*. This is what feminists claimed, rejecting, for the most part, Marx's and Marxists' materialism. Economy, according to feminists, does not explain all of society. Many, and even most, of the social phenomena produce themselves at the level of the superstructure of society, independently of its structural, economical level. These are *cultural* phenomena related to

8 Granted, however, the peculiarity of women's oppression.

the ways in which societies understand themselves. In this regard, patriarchy is the social phenomenon constituting women not as an economic object, but as a cultural one. More precisely, patriarchy is the system under which women are culturally constructed as a socially oppressed group; the politicisation of sexuality largely becomes now the disclosure of the process through which women's self-conception is socially constructed by the way in which literature, habits, systems of education, myths, science, and so on, create the ideal woman.[9]

The rejection of materialism makes feminism quite different from Marxism. In Marxism, capitalism does certainly appear to be a dehumanising system. But the way in which this judgement has to be taken in Marxism is entirely descriptive (Wood 2004); there is no normative judgement in Marx's analysis of capitalism. Marxism is not a political theory. Indeed, for Marx, capitalism will collapse not because of anything that we should or could do, but because of its internal mechanism. Feminism, on the contrary, is all but a scientific theory.

Close to liberalism, feminism essentially remains a *political* theory. For feminists, there is no doubt that patriarchy is an unjust social system. There is no scientific detachment in feminism. Feminism aims to be both an explanation of women's constitution as an oppressed group *and* a *normative* programme for their liberation. Unlike liberalism, however, in second-wave feminism, women are not oppressed *individuals*. Patriarchy constructs women as an oppressed group. And only when women realise how patriarchy constructs them can they undertake a process of liberation, providing their own definitions of themselves *as women* and escaping the trap of individualism. This was the aim of self-awareness groups (MacKinnon 1989b). Self-awareness was meant to activate a process of consciousness raising, transforming women from an oppressed, socially constituted group into an active, self-identifying collective agent, able to define its own aims, interests, needs and desires.

However, the proper systematisation of both the analysis of women's oppression and the normative proposal for their liberation proved to be rather complicated for feminists. A theory of patriarchy had to be able to show that all women were oppressed as a socially constituted group. But what exactly did this mean? Was rich women's oppression the same as that of the poor? What needed to be said of black women's oppression in a racist society? Was there a theory able to encompass all of these differences?

To understand the importance of the question, it is essential to see how patriarchy aims to be a theory of society. Depending on what social

---

9 This is why it became common for feminist books to analyse romances, science, mythology (de Beauvoir 1953 [1949]; Millett 1991 [1977]).

divisions we see as most fundamental, we get different theories of society and different social objects or no object at all, as for individualists. This problem is not merely one of recent past. If perhaps the class question has declined with the decline of orthodox Marxism, the race question is still at the centre of the discussion, and we can trace many actual debates on identities and cultures back to it (Appiah 1990; Gutman 1994).

What could then encompass all women's differences and unify them into a group in the required sense? In answer to this question, some feminists directed their interests to a very peculiar form of naturalism. Liberal feminists, as we have seen, devoted all of their efforts to challenging the idea that women should be characterised by their natural capacity for giving birth. In some way, this was irrelevant. But some feminists saw this effort as misguided.[10] Agreeing, in a certain sense, with the anti-feminists' claim that those capacities are *essential* to women, they rejected the liberal feminists' assumption that we should look at them as just *accidental* characteristics of women. According to these feminists, because of women's capacity for giving birth, women have a variety of characteristics – moral, behavioural, relational – that make them profoundly different from men (Tronto 1994).[11] What is wrong with men's anti-feminist arguments is not that women are essentially different, because women are different from men; rather, it is the way in which these differences are considered (Jaggar 1983, pp. 93–98). All that men are not able to do, or cannot do as well as women, is deemed to be insignificant – something to laugh about. All that women are not able to do, or not able to do as well as men, is of the highest value. This is what patriarchy consists of: patriarchy is not the claim that women are different, but the claim that what makes them different has little value. The problem is in social meanings, not in the difference.

While there is certainly something appealing about the idea that the capacity for giving birth characterises women in certain respects, it also presents a number of difficulties. To start with, women's purported capacities didn't emerge clearly. Apart from commonplace trivia, what exactly are women's special talents and capacities? Secondly, is it actually so clear that the biological capacity for giving birth is connected with women's special moral and behavioural attitudes? And how exactly? What can be said of all those women who do not care about maternity? What of women who cannot have children? Are they somehow not truly women?[12]

---

10 De Beauvoir had already raised a similar point: see de Beauvoir (1991 [1977], pp. 50*ff*).
11 For morality, see Gilligan (1982); see also Benhabib (1986). On the connection between the ethics of care and naturalism, see Baier (1995).
12 Many authors interested in the perspective of the ethics of care try to detach it from a specifically feminist perspective: see Held (2006); Moller Okin (1989a, 1989b).

All of these objections are important points for this (somewhat) natural-istic view and have been raised by a number of feminists of all orientations. But the sharpest attack comes from a radical feminist conception whose perplexities do not depend mainly on how women's nature is specified. Even when they harshly criticise liberals and liberal feminism, second-wave feminists have never lost track of feminism as a *political* theory. Criticising society in the name of an untouched, pre-political reign during which women could find (or find again) their original nature makes feminism, according to such a view, no longer a political theory. Human beings have always lived in a political environment and, as far as we know, such a politi-cal environment has always been patriarchal (MacKinnon 1989b, p. 51).

Feminists have often looked at patriarchy as a system based on female domestic confinement. But, according to the more radical feminists, if we look at our patriarchal society, women's maternal role is not what primarily characterises them. When we look at society, what strikes us is how women, far from inhabiting a restrictive, perhaps, but also protective domestic envi-ronment, live their lives in a world of terror in which being beaten, killed, raped, harassed and sexually abused as prostitutes and in pornography is the norm (MacKinnon 1989a, p. 332).

This does not happen by chance. According to radical feminists, the majority of men who commit sexual crimes of different levels of serious-ness don't think they are doing something wrong, but that they are doing what women want or desire, manifesting what men believe sex simply is (MacKinnon 1989a, p. 318) Because men conceive women as a means for their own sexual satisfaction, they do not perceive the abusiveness of their sexual behaviour. This is finally what patriarchy is about. Patriarchy is nei-ther about the denial of women's full citizenship nor about their cultural devaluation. Those phenomena, important as they are, are only the effect of a deeper one: of women's sexualisation. Patriarchy is about the way in which men dominate women by sexualising them (MacKinnon 1989a, p. 315).

It is important to understand that saying that men dominate by sexualising women is quite different, and raises a more profound claim, than affirming that men try to place women's (naturally given) sexuality under male con-trol. One might think that, thanks to contraception, women are now free to have sex as men always have, pursuing only their pleasure and natural inclination. But, according to radical feminists, making sense of sexuality as a natural instinct or impulse that societies variously regulate (and often repress) is no less mistaken than glorifying maternity. There is no such natu-ral sexuality for them; no instinct or impulse or natural sexual desire ready to be enjoyed as soon as sexual liberation is achieved (MacKinnon 1989a, p. 320). On the contrary, sex is *in itself* a social construction. Heterosexuality and men's satisfaction are the constitutive norms of patriarchy. In other words, women are sexually free only insofar as they adopt (or adapt to) a sexuality socially modelled on male desire; this, in effect, renders women's subjection a good thing (MacKinnon 1989a, p. 322).

By insisting that patriarchy is not a system of (possibly unjust) norms regulating the sexual lives of different groups of people, but one that creates sexualities, radical feminists come very close to solving the problem we posed at the beginning: how can women exist as a social object? How can any social objects exist?

Women, eventually, are sexually defined, but sex itself is a social fact, not a natural, biological or metaphysical one. It is the very sexual difference that is socially constituted.

It must be noted that this conception of patriarchy is very demanding of women's sexual behaviour; as a consequence, no distinction is made between sex and violence (MacKinnon 1989a, p. 323). Yet, for many of us, it is very difficult to see the act of making love with the man we love with as an act of violence or to see any man as a rapist. Many of us would find it simply absurd to believe that, because of sexualisation, the pleasure we can feel in being wooed is nothing but the compliance of a slave and that super-rich top models are poor victims of a sexualised world. It's complicated. One could wonder if there is not some 'sex phobia' at play here.[13] One could wonder: what about women's freedom? And, in fact, many objections to radical feminism have been raised on liberal grounds, an exemplification of which is the recent debate on prostitution and pornography (Anderson 2002; Primoratz 1993). If, for radical feminists, both prostitution and pornography are two places in which male domination manifests itself in sexualised women, questions regarding freedom of choice are easily raised by liberals (MacKinnon 1989a, p. 327).[14] Who can say that prostitutes are there only as means for men's satisfaction? Maybe they like it too. Maybe it's a choice. To follow such a route would be easy for me, but this is not exactly what I want to do. Not directly, at least.

Radical feminists would certainly not be surprised by women's reactions to their theses. Obviously, women can (and will) protest that they love their men and do not feel as though they are living in a world of terror. This is the way in which social construction works. But, according to them, we cannot take what women say at face value because they possibly speak the words of societal norms, not their own (MacKinnon 1989a, p. 340). Under the surface of what they have been taught to think and to say, there can be – and,

---

13 For a defence against such an accusation and a different consideration of MacKinnon's theses, see Bernick (1992).
14 See also Dworkin (1991, 1998).

according to radical feminists, *there is* – the reality of their oppression. But hadn't liberal feminists said exactly the same?

When liberal feminists started their fight, the problem that they faced was that the large majority of women were at best indifferent to feminism and, if they cared to consider it, considered it a bunch of absurdities. But feminists didn't surrender there. They clarified how what appear to be people's preferences and wants may sometimes not be enough, and that it is important to take into account the history of those preferences and wants – that is, the conditions under which they were formed. But if so, then what exactly distinguishes liberal from radical feminists?

The answer, I think, is radical feminists' lack of any conception of individuals, together with an unreasonable faith in the power of consciousness raising. Radical feminists are not wrong because they don't take what women want seriously. Sometimes, we have very good reasons for not taking wants this seriously. Radical feminists are wrong because they don't take *any* women's wants or desires seriously. In their iconoclastic battle against naturalism, radical feminists have ended up refusing to specify *any* theory of the individual – which leaves us unable to evaluate what we should and what we shouldn't take into account and on which bases. Radicalising the idea of social construction as not naturally grounded, radical feminism makes it impossible to understand how to modify our constructions as soon as we realise they don't work. In so doing, however, radical feminists sway between two different senses in which social constructions can be taken. To say that something is a social construction, in fact, can be taken to mean that certain social criteria are used to classify individuals into a certain group. In that regard, those criteria have the value they have. They can be criticised and rejected, as soon as they don't work or as soon as better criteria are found. But it can also be taken to mean something deeper than this. As soon as we refuse to explain the why and how we have such social constructions, all that we can say is that we have them, that they specify our identities. Once this is done, however, the only way in which women might reclaim themselves from their social construction is by invoking some deep essence they might find inside themselves.

But legitimate suspicion might arise on both the rationale of the enterprise and the radical feminists' successful vindication of it. Radical feminists want feminism to provide a general theory of sexuality within the framework of patriarchy, thereby making feminism an encompassing theory of sexuality. But all that they seem to say is that patriarchy is just there: you need only look to find women who are beaten, raped or harassed. Data, however, are not theories. The way in which women's lives are represented; their victimisation; the way in which sexual groups are stereotyped: all seem aimed at replacing facts with theories, by concealing weaknesses at the theoretical level.

Let me conclude this chapter with one last remark. Radical feminists criticise liberal feminism as nothing but classical liberalism *applied* to women; only radical feminism is unqualified feminism (MacKinnon 1989b, p. 117). I agree. Even if liberal feminism did not amount to an 'add women and stir' formula, as we have seen, it remains true that liberal feminists thought of liberal anti-feminist theses as inconsistencies, resulting from the prejudices of philosophers. Liberalism was their theory; feminism was their fight. As a fight, liberal feminism in not engaged in a theory of sexuality. From a liberal (feminist) point of view, social-sexual groups are only individuals (possibly wrongly) categorised in certain ways. Rejecting those categories leaves people free to enjoy whatever sex they like.

Radical feminists wanted feminism to be more than a fight. They wanted feminism to be a theory. As we have seen, this required a theory of patriarchy that radical feminists were unable to adequately provide. If this is true, the failure of radical feminism is the failure of feminism as a theoretical enterprise, which I think is the case. Feminism, ultimately, didn't prove able to provide reasons for believing that women *as women* exist. As a theory, it lacks an object.

Shaping a theory of their own has been an understandably marvellous enterprise for a couple of generations of philosophers. But, finally, we have to say that it didn't work. Feminism has essentially been a movement, not a theory, and even less a general theory of sexuality. Feminists should recognise this. The attempt to keep feminism alive as a theory risks playing a regressive role now, by keeping alive an old theory of patriarchy and reinforcing gender divisions that no longer have reason to exist.

References

ANDERSON Scott A., "Prostitution and Sexual Autonomy: Making Sense of the Prohibition of Prostitution," *Ethics*, no. 4 (July 2002), 748–780.

APPIAH Antony, "'But Would That Still Be Me?' Notes on Gender, 'Race', Ethnicity, as Sources of 'Identity'." *The Journal of Philosophy*, no. 10 (October 1990), 493–499.

BAIER Annette, *Moral Prejudices: Essays on Ethics* (Cambridge, MA: Harvard University Press, 1995).

BENHABIB Seyla, "The Generalized and the Concrete Other: The Kholberg/Gilligan Debate," *Praxis International*, no. 4 (January 1986), 402–424.

BERNICK Susan, "The Logic of the Development of Feminism: or, Is MacKinnon to Feminism as Parmenides Is to Greek Philosophy?," *Hypatia*, no. 1 (February 1992), 1–15.

DE BEAUVOIR Simone, *The Second Sex* (London: Jonathan Cape, 1953 [1949]).

DWORKIN Andrea, *Mercy* (New York: Four Walls Eight Windows, 1991).

DWORKIN Andrea, "Pornography and Grief," in *Letters from a War Zone: Writings 1976–1989* (New York: Dutton, 1998).

ENGELS Friedrich, *The Origin of the Family, Private Property, and the State* (London: Penguin, 2010 [1884]).

FARRELLY Colin, "Patriarchy and Historical Materialism," *Hypatia*, no. 1 (Winter 2011), 1–21.

FRIEDAN Betty, *The Feminine Mystique* (London: Penguin, 2010 [1963]).

GILLIGAN Carol, *In a Different Voice*, (Cambridge, MA: Harvard University Press, 1982).

GUTMAN Amy, ed., *Multiculturalism: Examining the Politics of Recognition* (Princeton, NJ: Princeton University Press, 1994).

HAINES Bridged, "Beyond Patriarchy: Marxism, Feminism, and Elfriede Jelinek 'Die Liebhaberinnen'," *Modern Language Review*, no. 3 (July 1997), 643–655.

HELD Virginia, *The Ethics of Care: Personal, Political, Global* (Oxford: Oxford University Press, 2006).

JAGGAR Alison M., *Feminist Politics and Human Nature* (Lanham, MD: Rowman & Littlefield, 1983).

MacKINNON Catherine, "Sexuality, Pornography, and Method: 'Pleasure under Patriarchy'," *Ethics*, no. 2 (January 1989a), 314–346.

MacKINNON Catherine, *Toward a Feminist Theory of the State* (Cambridge, MA: Harvard University Press, 1989b).

MILL John Stuart, "The Subjugation of Women," in *"On Liberty" and Other Writings* (Cambridge: Cambridge University Press, 1995 [1869]).

MILLETT Kate, *Sexual Politics* (London: Virago Press, 1991 [1977]).

MOLLER OKIN Susan, *Justice, Gender, and the Family* (New York: Basic Books, 1989a).

MOLLER OKIN Susan, "Reason and Feelings in Thinking about Justice," *Ethics*, no. 2 (January 1989b), 229–249.

PHILLIPS Anne, *Feminism and Politics* (Oxford: Oxford University Press, 1998).

PRIMORATZ Igor, "What's Wrong with Prostitution?," *Philosophy*, no. 264 (April 1993), 159–182.

TRONTO Joan, *Moral Boundaries: A Political Argument for an Ethic of Care* (London: Routledge, 1994).

WOLLSTONECRAFT Mary, *A Vindication of the Rights of Women* (Mineola, NY: Dover, 1996 [1792]).

WOOD Allen, *Marx* (London: Routledge, 2004).

2 Exponential territorialization

Reduce, refuse or reuse? An exploration of the territories of inclusive legal norms and gender binary

Valeria Venditti

This chapter draws on Deleuze's and Guattari's notion of territory to evaluate the effects and results of the mutual interaction between legal norms and gender standards. More specifically, it is concerned with assessing the social reverberation of legal measures that aim at challenging the marginalization of those people who are discriminated against on the basis of their nonconformity with gendered standards.

Law deals with gender in many ways: from the legitimation of same-sex unions, to the regulation of gender reassignment procedure, up to the allocation of female quotas. However, although gender-based discrimination takes many forms and concerns many different situations, a specific mode to legally address these problems has been privileged in the last decades: inclusion started to appear as the most suitable solution to respond to problems of social injustice and inequality. Mostly perceived as a way of promoting the adjustment of an obsolete legal body to new forms of living, inclusion proceeds mainly by the extension of existing rights to people whose discrimination is linked with questions of gender. Yet this adjustment is always and already a twofold one, governed by the collision of powers and forces. In this sense, while the legislator operates with the best intents to face marginalization, it also rearticulates meanings that have to do with gender, stabilizing and ratifying some of them, while excluding others.

In what follows, I will portray this inclusive turn as an inherently conservative one—a process that curbs differences through the annexation of nonconforming elements into the accepted symbolical domain of gendered practices. Namely, I will consider "gender-sensitive" regulations as reterritorializing processes that, by including nonconforming gender identities/relationships into a traditional matrix, normalize them and obliterate their deterritorializing force. My claim is that inclusive policies (no matter how progressive or disruptive) are inclined to perpetrate an understanding of gender roles and social relationships that concurs to reinforce the symbolical weight of gender binary. This happens because both law and gender are territorializing forces, whose conjunction eventuates in an "exponential re-territorialization," which cannot be overcome from an extralegal position (an antinormative instance that refuses legal inclusion, which I will call the "refuse" approach) nor from an intralegal one (a strategic embracement of policies so as to change them, which I will call the "reuse" approach).

To do so, I will look at the legalization of same-sex marriage as an instance of those legal norms that somehow challenge the traditional positioning of gendered bodies into society. The legitimation of same-sex unions provides a glaring (and by now classic) example of the ambiguity of inclusive strategies: in endowing same-sex couples with marital rights, the institution of marriage keeps its function and structure intact, while enlarging the spectrum of those who can benefit from legal recognition. In this sense, nonheterosexual couples gain access not only to certain rights and benefits, but also to a symbolic structure based on ideas of coupledom, monogamy, familial ties, and all those features that traditionally characterize marriage. Marriage becomes the reterritorializing device—the "birdsong," as Deleuze would have it—that perimeters the spectrum of thinkable relationships, recollocating alternative gendered practices within the "territory" of social accepted standards.

After a brief explanation of the concept of territory, as proposed by Deleuze and Guattari (1987), and a little detour through the awkward unpredictability of human affective relationships, I will delve into the analysis of inclusive legal measures by parsing three different perspectives on inclusion: *reuse, refuse, reduce*. In the conclusion, I will go back to the concept of territory to demonstrate the link between inclusive legal measures and gender binary.

Territories

The concept of territory emerges in many sites of Deleuze's and Guattari's work. Although it never comes to be thoroughly defined, this notion appears as a multivocal, polyphonic concept, which finds application in many different contexts. Territory is a demarcated and closed space, either physical or not, contingent on a cluster of operations that delineates its structure and maintains its internal order. While a territory comes to be configured as a stable entity, its order is an oscillating one. The dynamism that affects territories is functional, since stability originates from the alternation of destabilization and rebalance, where the former is the natural flourishing of movements that threaten stability itself and the latter is the effort to tame them, to bring them back to "neutral."

A territory comes to be outlined as a stable, defined (and thus *safe*) space. The task of *territorialization* consists in organizing a series of objects around a center through "an activity of selection, elimination and extraction" that "take[s] something from chaos" (Deleuze and Guattari 1987: 312). Through this process, new territories, with their internal orders and "directional components" (Deleuze and Guattari 1987: 314), are drawn from "the chaotic indeterminacy of the real" and put in relation with other framed spaces. In this sense, territorialization gives "rise to the creation of networks, planes, zones of cohesion, which do not map this chaos so much as draw strength, force, material from it for a provisional and open-ended cohesion, temporary modes of ordering, slowing, filtering" (Grosz 2008: 8). Such "cohesions," or assemblages, compose a code: an internal set of unwritten customary norms that internally organize the partial components of the framed object, while determining its relations with other, external, objects. It is possible to say, then, that a territory is a space that *allows* the rise of certain sensations, meanings, bonds or directions, or the achievement of certain goals—that is, the transformation of a given situation. It is the structure of the territory—how meanings and objects are disposed within it—that, literally, creates the space for these "things," these events, to happen.

Yet every territory, no matter how stable it appears, might unfold again into chaos, going through a process of deterritorialization. While framing was "the means by which the plane of composition composes," deterritorialization is the moment "of upheaval and transformation" (Grosz 2008: 13). As I noted above, destabilization is a constitutive moment. At this juncture, the features that mark the territory tend to crumble. Deterritorialization is the emersion of new core features or the dissolution of old ones within the same territory. In this moment, another distribution of the space is set; the boundaries of the territory are reorganized around a new center or in accordance with new internal forces. This arrangement is reterritorialization, the necessary reframing of the space to save the stability of the space itself.[1]

This mechanism, the swinging order of territorialization, can be observed in territories such as political communities. These spaces are built via homogenization—that is, via the delineation of well-defined boundaries (physical and normative), and the promotion of shared values and standards.

Institutions, laws, and customary norms can be seen as tools for the stabilization of such a territory. First, they function as primary signs (marking meanings and drawing boundaries) for the construction of the territory.

---

1 As an example of a dynamics that breaks the order of a territory, we can think of the transformation of the identity "woman" after the rise of feminist movements and the achievement of other political and social changes. We might also focus on the ways in which women's liberation has been followed by a linguistic, symbolic, and political process of reterritorialization, aimed at recollocating women within the boundaries of a highly regulated binary system.

Additionally, they intervene in the redistribution of internal spaces and lines, networks and directions. They can, in other words, trigger processes of reterritorialization.

Inclusive legal policies are remarkable examples of reterritorializing forces. Their aim is social inclusion, a process through which marginalized or excluded social elements are reintegrated, accepted in the boundaries of the territory.

For the purposes of this chapter, I will focus on one specific aspect of inclusion, reading it as a saturating process, rather than as an "expansive" one. In this perspective, inclusion proceeds by adding people who do not fit shared standards into recognized grids of meaning. Seldom is it realized through the modification, the expansion, of the grids themselves; rather, it operates on dissonant entities, on those elements of the territory that might threaten its boundaries. Inclusive legal policies serve the scope of organizing a social realm by means of distinctions, to stabilize it, by addressing nonconforming social elements that come to be "made" consistent with accepted social norms. The legal recognition of same-sex marriages illustrates this dynamics. When same-sex couples (nonconforming social elements that might threaten stability[2]) are endowed with the right to access the marriage institution, they are invited to *become appropriate*, to *fit* a well-defined schema. In shifting from being the recognition of the union between a man and a woman in a personal relationship to become the recognition of the union between two people either of different sexes or of the same sex in a personal relationship, marriage keeps its basic structure. On the contrary, the same-sex relationship undergoes a far more dramatic change. Historically, gay men and lesbian women have organized their relationships in ways that do not match the traditional framework of the heterosexual couple.[3] The eccentric promiscuity of the gay man and the rizhomatic domesticity of lesbian sexuality find no room in the welcoming institutions. Through legitimization, the nontraditional practices of the self, of care, as well as the delineation of alternative ways of living (not based on nuclear families, monogamy, coupledom), gives way to the neat acceptance of *a standard* of living.

In this perspective, it is possible to see the merit of legal recognition in securing both the integration of marginalized people and the stability of the institution that their sexual conducts threatened. In being no longer exposed to the risk of discrimination, lesbian and gay couples cease to expose the institution/marriage (a territory in itself) to the risk of

---

2 On this, see Bersani (1995); Seidman (1993); Croce (2015a).
3 See, e.g., Chasin (2001); Cobb (2011); Croce (2015c); Warner (2000).

collapse. By means of reconfiguring marriage ever so slightly, law reterritorializes a cluster of dynamics that might deeply destabilize the social order of a community.

Spaces

To understand the deterritorializing impact of nonheterosexualized sexual conducts, it is important to consider same-sex relationships as forces that open up the way for new meanings, sensations, ideas. Sexual conducts function as sub-territories of the larger territory of a social community: they display embodied standards and personify social values. Above all, they offer spaces in which to develop needs and desires, and to express and assess them.

Within a relationship, an organism extracts "from the external world the elements which will satisfy its tendencies and needs" (Deleuze 2004: 19). However, "forms of . . . sexual attraction, affirm the excessiveness of the body and the natural order, their capacity to . . . enter into becomings that transform each"; relationships are not "homeostatic relation of stabilization, . . . but a fundamentally dynamic, awkward, mal-adaptation that enables the production of the frivolous, the unnecessary, the pleasing, the sensory for their own sake" (Grosz 2008: 7). In this sense, relationships are mines of experiences and melting pots of ideas. Thus they are very unstable objects that call for the need to institute an "original world" that can mediate "between [a subject's] tendencies and the external milieu, developing artificial means of satisfaction . . . [which] liberate an organism from nature though they subject it to something else, transforming tendencies by introducing them into a new milieu" (Deleuze 2004: 19). These artificial means are, according to Deleuze, institutions. Interestingly, law is only one way of sanctioning and enforcing these mediators (granting them continuity and operationality), since there are other, customary, forms in which institutions comes to be imposed.[4] Traditions and common knowledge, often enfolded in what can be defined as a *habitus* (Bourdieu 2001), along with clusters of sedimented meanings and accepted models, channel these institutions through a nonwritten, less straightforward path.

Gender categories are certainly to be considered an element of this subtler sedimentation. Like every institution, they represent cultural objects that organize and stabilize—*territorialize*—the chaotic substance of the social realm. By means of a constant labeling, gender categories divide the social realm, instituting spaces in which desires, needs, and tendencies might

4 See Deleuze and Guattari (1988: 312).

unfold. I have already observed that territories allow for certain meanings to emerge, precluding others. Accordingly, gender categories offer the possibility to develop certain lines, but at the same time are always—virtually and actually—excluding other ones, which become *unspeakable*, even *unthinkable*, in that very context.

Now, two things should be observed: on the one hand, gender categories set in motion processes of territorialization and reterritorialization as inclusive laws do. In this sense, inclusive legal measures that operate with gender categories can somehow be seen as "exponential territorializer." The connection of the two institutions produces a form of territorialization that joins together a cluster of differentiating concepts (male/female) and a series of dividing procedures (what is in/what is out), both implementing a twofold organization of the elements in a territory. Inclusive legal norms concerning gender transcode the territorializing impact of gender into more rigid and less malleable entities. This transcoding "is not a simple addition, but the constitution of a new plane, as of a surplus value" (Deleuze and Guattari 1987: 315). Legal norms ratify and enforce the horizons of possibilities opened up by gender categories. This means, as I will explain below, that norms replicate the structure delineated by gender categories. Yet, at the same time, "juridification" (Venditti 2016) of gender categories allows for the articulation of desires and needs that differ from those virtually formulable within a social context ruled by nonjuridified gender norms (Butler 1997).

Again, it is possible to take same-sex marriage as an example. I have shown above that the inclusion of same-sex couples into marriage only partially modifies the grid of meanings that the institution of marriage composes.[5] To put it another way, it is more likely for the legal institution to change the same-sex relationships in which it intervenes than for the opposite to be true. In turn, however, gender categories embedded in the law inform the way in which relationships are articulated. Here, the double bind of exponential territorialization becomes manifest. The inclusive force reterritorializes nonconforming relationships, inviting them to embrace a nondestabilizing style of living (marriage instead of promiscuity, motherhood instead of sisterhood). Meanwhile, gender standards make available certain "slots" for desires and needs, offering a finite set of nuances to coloring marriage: traditions—a certain division of roles, certain aspirations and expectations—infiltrate the lifestyle of even a nontraditional married couple. In this scenario, little or no leeway is left for the deterritorializing experience of alternative affective relationships:

5 See Croce (2015b).

all of the bubbling forces that ferment in the unbearable contingency of actual intercourses (Berlant and Edelman 2013) fade under the spotlight of the institutional codification of accepted meanings and the echoing of gender binary.

Domains

If the idea of an exponential reterritorialization might already sound incredibly claustrophobic (a sort of Schengen area that totalizes relationships without visible boundaries), here comes the bad news.

The conjunction of law and gender binary not only tends to saturate alternative affective relationships, taming their deterritorializing force; it also composes a very steady territory. As I will explain, the double bind of an exponential reterritorialization eludes any critical attempt to trouble the subtle mechanism triggered by institutions. This happens because a territory tends to define its own boundaries as edges that mark the space of *intelligible* concepts. In other words, when deterritorialization has to take place within a given set of meanings, it can only *be conceived through these meanings*. Concepts and notions that come to be articulated in a territory lose their destabilizing momentum because *they comply with the grid of meanings available in the structure* (Bourdieu 2001; Butler 1997). Being inside the structure *is* being exposed to reterritorialization. A proof of this fateful drowning can be found in the carousel of critical voices for or against same-sex marriage, which—despite their bold theoretical stance—are inherently doomed to leave intact the normalizing force exerted by inclusive gender norms. More precisely, the conjunction of the two territorializing forces (law and gender) can be neither opposed from an extralegal position (by refusing inclusive policies) nor modified by an intralegal one (by strategically embracing policies to change them). Since its strength resides precisely in the exponential reproduction of a given system, both embracement and denial occur within the boundaries of the territory, recognizing and remarking them.

It is possible to grasp this dynamic by looking at three (or, more aptly, one plus two) general approaches to the legitimation of same-sex unions. I propose to call them *reduce, refuse*, and *reuse*. *Reduce* is not a problematic position. Reducers welcome inclusion for what it is and are willing to adopt a mainstream form of living, because this constitutes the linear path towards a more equal society. In this way, they "reduce" their identities and interactions to pre-given recognized standards and, in turn, receive a series of rights and privileges from which they were excluded before. This position bears no deterritorializing traits; it displays only the reterritorializing movement at work, without any counterforce to oppose it.

On the contrary, *refusers* and *reusers* operate critically on patterns proposed by inclusive norms. The former group wholeheartedly opposes inclusion, perceiving it as a removal of differences through normalization. Authors such as Leo Bersani (1995), Lee Edelman (2004), and Michael Warner (2000) have largely condemned the process of erasure that inclusive legal norms set in motion.[6] In particular, they lament that recognition carries with it the eradication of alternative drives (a flair for extinction, a passion for dissipation, an appetite for queerness) that find no space in the heterosexual, reproductive linear path delineated by institutions. Inclusion wipes away nonconforming forms of living, thus—refusers say—is not a real solution, but only another way of being socially excluded. Despite the strong opposition, though, the refusers' approach can be articulated only in relation to the inclusive process they reject. Refusers are engaged in a struggle that *requires* the enemy. The nonconforming identity is *tailored on* the *reversal* of territorialized categories, so that it appears to be contingent on it.[7] Refusers operate by rejecting the possibility of becoming a part of a territory, but in doing so they act as perfect instruments of reterritorialization: they ostensibly embody the outsider. In doing so, they mark the boundaries of the territory by laying outside them.[8]

Finally, the supporters of the third approach, *reuse*, also consider inclusion to be a flattening tool that can actually lead to an eradication of differences. However, their position is an eccentric one, since reusers endorse a strategic use of inclusive policies. Among others,[9] Judith Butler (1990, 2004) suggests that juridified identities can be adopted to change conservative categories "from within." In this view, an actor can strategically embrace a legal category to benefit from social recognition, then change the social and symbolic meaning of this category through her own *performance*. It is by embodying a category, reusers contend, that single conducts might *reverse* the legal demand to fit standards through a form of appropriation, a sort of inverse colonization of the mainstream system. However, attention should be paid to the risks that identification with legal requirements carries with it (Butler 2004: 75–101). At first sight, exploiting legal categories to access privileges without expressively changing one's own conduct or endorsing certain standards

---

6 A great panoramic of these position is offered in Bernini (2016).
7 I cannot analyze here this flipside of negative politics. On this, see Braidotti (2011), in particular Pt IV.
8 The outsider as the one who constitutes normality has been inquired by many authors: see, among others, Bourdieu (2001).
9 See, e.g., Bernstein (1997); Leckey (2011a, 2011b).

seems perfectly possible.[10] Yet it must be considered that subjects might not always be in control of their individual performances, because the meanings they operate with exceed single signifiers (the ones we create through our actions, gestures, speeches), looming over a subject's arbitrary decision. Individual strategies overlap with a cluster of powers[11] that is already at work before and beyond the subject's critical engagement with any of the categories ratified by the law.

Again: personal desires, needs, and tendencies come to be shaped inside the box of signifiers into which the subject might tap. In *traversing a territory*, social actors are not only *navigating* through the assemblage of meanings that composes it, but also *negotiating* their instincts with the institutions that structure and organize those meanings in a more stable way: "In other words, every individual experience presupposes, as an *a priori*, the existence of a milieu in which that experience is conducted, a species-specific milieu or an institutional milieu" (Deleuze 2004: 19). What the reuse approach does not take into account is the innate swarming of instincts into institutions and the consequent adaptation of the former to the latter. Institutions, Deleuze (2004: 19–20) explains, are spaces in which tendencies find "ready-made" forms of satisfaction;[12] yet, "if it is true that tendencies are satisfied by the institution, the institution is not explained by tendencies," since "same sexual needs will never explain the multiple possible forms of marriage . . . because there are a thousand other . . . procedures of satisfaction—and the tendencies satisfied by such procedures neither trigger nor determine the procedures." In other words, institutions channel the countless number of tendencies that might originate from human intercourses in one (maybe more, yet always countable) single, well-recognizable, and accepted relationship. If this is so, it is possible to see the limits of the third approach I am inquiring here: that being engaged in a marriage—no matter how detached and aware, critical and lucid we are—requires the use of meanings that do

---

10 Besides Butler's analysis (devoted to transsexual people and gender identity disorder), it is possible to take the case of "marriages of interest" celebrated between citizens of a nation and refugees/aliens so that the latter can gain citizenship. In this case, as Éric Fassin has recently inquired, an entire new rhetoric around homosexuality and homosexual behaviors emerges: see, in general, Fassin (2003).

11 The legal power that legitimizes; the symbolical power that structures; the linguistic power that recognizes. On this, see Butler and Venditti (2014: 93–395); Haslanger (2012: 113–138).

12 Institutions, in fact, offer answers to those conducts or behaviors that might pose a problem or require an endless negotiation. In providing an example, Deleuze (2004: 19) observes that "money will liberate you from hunger . . . and marriage will spare you from searching out a partner."

not belong to a single relationship, but inform the very possibility of being engaged in *that type of relationship*, of defining one's own condition *through* that institutionalized bond. Here lies the slippery slope of inclusive mechanisms: the disguised counter-conduct promoted by reusers (exploitation with no further implications) might turn out to be a passive—thought unwilling—embrace of social standards and norms. That is, it may favor the process of reterritorialization of the awkward, unstable objects that relationships are.

Grounds

Although the approaches I have analyzed adopt different strategies, refusers and reusers share a common weakness that prevents them from undertaking any effective perturbation on the mechanism of "exponential reterritorialization." The impossibility of overcoming the process of reterritorialization set in motion by inclusive legal policies concerning gender inheres in the very collocation of these two critical approaches: they operate with the tools offered by legal norms and gender standards, within a given system.

As the law rearticulates the territorializing meanings of gender by locating them in a territorializing structure, refusers and reusers are doomed to replicate such territorializing instances, even when trying to dismantle them. By drawing on Butler (1997: 84*ff*), it is possible to observe that both refusers and reusers are prompted to "recontexualize" the twofold bond forged by inclusive policies and gender standards. In taking up meanings and signifiers embedded in them, this recontextualization "occasions a reversal" that, instead of banishing or changing the inclusive and the binary discourses, "proliferates" them. Refusers replicate these discourses to deny them; reusers, to alter them. Nonetheless, both parties incite their "recirculation" and, above all, recognize its authority.

Going back to the notion of territory, we can see how the replication of a discourse, which always denotes the recognition of its authority,[13] matches the process of stabilization that precedes reterritorialization. The delineation of a battlefield (the territory circumscribed by legal and social institutions) already defines the boundaries of the dispute itself. To mark the space implies a precise implication of the possibilities at stake—that is, it shapes the cluster of virtual opportunities that social actors have within that territory, by making *specific meanings* available. On the one hand, these meanings inform desires and needs; on the other, they channel and organize drive and tendency. In this perspective, exponential territorialization

---

13 Since it presupposes a subjection, a recognition, of the value of the discourse itself.

appears in all of its strength: the gender binary imposes social meanings; it territorializes gender relations by marking the lines along which relationships can unfold. Male and female (regardless of how many variations they have[14]) are the central features to which affective desires and needs are prompted to conform. Meanwhile, inclusive legal policies arrange the messy variety of tendencies in clear-cut institutions, channeling the virtual thinkability of other affective configurations. By playing with these discourses and using their lexicon and jargon, critical voices are neutralized, reabsorbed in the circumscribed perimeter of the territory, subjected to its forces. Destabilization in these contexts is always followed by reterritorialization: refusers are cast out, re-exposed to marginalization, since their voices remain *outside* the political debate, to be shelved in the rarefied realm of cultural studies. Reusers, in turn, reluctantly join the system. Yet reluctance does not produce new forms of living nor does it open up the way to an imagining of new institutions; it is only a poke—a Socratic bell—a critical approach to politics that negotiates between benefits and dissatisfactions, still navigating in the safe waters of recognition.

The aim of this chapter was to consider and assess the status and value of critical approaches meant to rearticulate the traditional matrix within which our affective relationships come to be shaped. The notion of territory proved to be a useful tool to give an account of the resilience of certain practices and their effects on individual conducts and tendencies. Even if, in this view, the powerful bond between inclusive policies and gender binary appears to be a totalizing one, above all, when read in comparison with the ineffective counter-measures that critical approaches propose, the notion of territory also supplies us with a way out. As I have already noticed, a territory is not an ever-stable entity; it can unfold into chaos again. However, to unfold into chaos, it requires the intervention of disruptive forces that are capable of eluding reterritorialization.

References

Berlant, L., and Edelman, L. 2013. *Sex or the Unbearable*, Durham, NC, and London: Duke University Press.

Bernini, L. 2016. *Le Teorie Queer. Un'introduzione*, Milan: Mimesis.

Bernstein, M. 1997. Celebration and suppression: the strategic uses of identity by the lesbian and gay movement, *American Journal of Sociology*, vol. 103, no. 3, pp. 531–565.

Bersani, L. 1995. *Homos*, Cambridge, MA, and London: Harvard University Press.

---

14 A binary system absorbs all nonconforming gendered experiences: see the cases of transsexual people and hermaphrodite in Butler (1990, 2004).

Bourdieu, P. 2001. *Masculine Domination*, Stanford, CA: Stanford University Press.

Braidotti, R. 2011. *Nomadic Theory: The Portable Rosi Braidotti*, New York: Columbia University Press.

Butler, J. 1990. *Gender Trouble: Feminism and the Subversion of Identity*, London and New York: Routledge.

Butler, J. 1997. *Excitable Speech: A Politics of the Performative*, London and New York: Routledge.

Butler, J. 2004. *Undoing Gender*, London and New York: Routledge.

Butler, J., and Venditti, V. 2014. Reframing the normal, diffracting the norm: an interview with Judith Butler, *Politica & Società*, vol. 3, pp. 393–404.

Chasin, A. 2001. *Selling Out: The Gay and Lesbian Movement Goes to Market*, London: Palgrave Macmillan.

Cobb, M. 2011. Lonely, in J.E. Halley and A. Parker (eds), *After Sex: On Writing since Queer Theory*, Durham, NC, and London: Duke University Press, pp. 207–220.

Croce, M. 2015a. Homonormative dynamics and the subversion of culture, *European Journal of Social Theory*, vol. 18, no. 1, pp. 3–20.

Croce, M. 2015b. Secularization, legal pluralism, and the question of relationship-recognition regimes. *The European Legacy: Toward New Paradigms*, vol. 20, no. 2, pp. 151–165.

Croce, M. 2015c. From gay liberation to marriage equality: a political lesson to be learnt. *European Journal of Political Theory*, 16 April, online at http://journals.sagepub.com/doi/abs/10.1177/1474885115581425

Deleuze, G. 2004. *Desert Island and Other Texts 1953–1974*, Cambridge, MA, and London: Semiotext(e).

Deleuze, G., and Guattari, F. 1987. *A Thousand Plateaus, Capitalism and Schizophrenia*, Minneapolis, MN, and London: University of Minnesota Press.

Edelman, L. 2004. *No Future: Queer Theory and the Death Drive*, Durham, NC, and London: Duke University Press.

Fassin, É. 2003. L'inversion de la question homosexuelle. *Revue française de psychanalyse*, vol. 67, no. 1, pp. 263–284.

Grosz, E. 2008. *Chaos, Territory, Art: Deleuze and the Framing of the Earth*, New York: Columbia University Press.

Haslanger, S. 2012. *Resisting Reality: Social Construction and Social Critique*, New York: Oxford University Press.

Leckey, R. 2011a. Law reform, lesbian parenting, and the reflective claim. *Social & Legal Studies*, vol. 20, no. 3, pp. 331–348.

Leckey, R. 2011b. Lesbian parental projects in word and deed. *Revue juridique thémis*, vol. 45, pp. 315–341.

Seidman, S. 1993. *Fear of a Queer Planet: Queer Politics and Social Theory*, Minneapolis, MN: University of Minnesota Press.

Venditti, V. 2016. Millennials rights: politics on the lam. *Politica & Società*, vol. 2, pp. 169–188.

Warner, M. 2000. *The Trouble with Normal*, Cambridge, MA: Harvard University Press.

3 Can human rights exist without gender?

LGBTQI issues and the Council of Europe

Francesca Romana Ammaturo

Introduction: a contemporary problem for an ageless debate

Human rights are strong political currency for the globalised world in which we live. Yet this powerful language and instrument for empowerment and social change can often show its limitations, particularly when seen through the lenses of multifarious power relations emerging at the local, regional and global levels. In this context, the increasing legitimisation and inclusion of issues relating to sexual orientation and gender identity in the international human rights arena since the 1990s has opened up the space for questioning the fundamentally heteronormative matrix of society. At the same time, these developments have also created the opportunity to radically rethink the gender binary and the impact that this may have on both society and individual lives. In most cases, however, human rights discourses on issues relating to sexual orientation and gender identity at both the regional (take the case of the Council of Europe) and the different domestic levels have, so far, focused on a grand strategy of assimilation and taming of sexual and gender difference.

What mainstream human rights strategies have neglected (or failed to do) has been challenging given the institutions (the state, the family, the school, politics) that are conducive of the reproduction of these constraining frameworks of expression for individual experiences and constellations of sexual and emotional desires, as well as configurations of gender identity and gender expressions. Such a problem, commonly framed by queer (legal) theorists and scholars (Warner 1993; Valdes 1997; Fineman, Jackson, and Romero 2009), poses a fundamental challenge to human rights as a discipline. The underlying question is whether we can embrace fluidity and call for a system of human rights that is both adaptive to individual needs and experiences and comprehensive in its contemplation of the possible human rights issues connected to sex, sexuality and gender.

Elsewhere,[1] I have reflected on this challenging question that forces us to confront not only our conception of "human rights", but also our own conception of what a (gendered and sexed) "citizen" is. This is because claiming one's human rights without resorting to political action, following Arendt (2013), can be configured as a request to be made passive *objects* of human rights protection, rather than active *subjects* of international human rights law. Such a shift from (political) *inactivity* to *activity* can be conceptualised, however, only if we introduce the concept of citizenship into our analysis of human rights. In this regard, therefore, I have looked at the case law of the European Commission, and then Court, of Human Rights (ECommHR/ECtHR) relating to issues of sexual orientation and gender identity from a critical standpoint.

The genealogy of contemporary sexual citizenship needs to be traced beyond the framework of liberal assimilation and normalisation of lesbian, gay, bisexual, trans, queer and intersex (LGBTQI) and queer identities. This endeavour is based on an understanding of citizenship as an elective practice, rather than the mere possession of a given passport that opens up the opportunity to talk about "multi-sexual" and "multi-gender" sexual citizenship – that is, forms of citizenship that are, simultaneously, multi-scalar and multi-directional (Ammaturo 2017). In particular, "multi-sexual" and "multi-gendered" conceptions of citizenship allow the accommodation of non-linear configurations of sexuality and gender that escape the matrix of both heteronormativity and gender binarism within the domain of human rights. Ultimately, this framework of analysis calls for an approach to human rights that is more "bottom-up" than "top-down", insofar as it attempts to mould the codification, guarantee and protection of human rights principles after the concrete needs of the individual, rather than after a stylised and abstract universal subject of human rights.

At a glance, the call for an approach to human rights that is to be based on principles of fluidity, flexibility and accommodation seems to point in the direction of queer theory as both a theoretical and methodological tool of analysis. Finding a productive and satisfying synthesis between human rights and queer theory, however, may prove particularly difficult. If we adopt Kepros' definition (in Fineman et al. 2009, 5), for whom queer theory "fosters social change by keeping its own status as a theory undefined, its techniques post-modern, and its membership open", it becomes apparent that there may be dissonance with the characteristics of the liberal legal tradition, which emphasises instead objectivity, legitimacy, rationality and predictability. In the context of socio-legal research on human rights,

---

1 See Ammaturo (2017).

therefore, a different productive configuration of queer theory needs to be sought, mostly in the form of a strategic deployment of its most paradigmatic tenets, rather than in a systematic fashion. What can thus be achieved is the enacting of "transgressive readings of the corpus of legal knowledge, its tenets and other forms of discourse", as Moran (1996, 40) has suggested. When asking whether human rights can exist without or beyond gender, therefore, we are fundamentally interrogating queer theory, whilst acknowledging its fundamental limitations in the normative field. The compromise is thus constituted by introducing elements of critical legal theory and the Dworkian principle of interpreting legal texts that help us to engage with notions of power and power relations, the specific usages of legal language and the positionality of legal actors (Dworkin 1982, 1986).

Once this preliminary theoretical and methodological question has been addressed, it is possible to move on to the problematisation of the necessity of "gendering" or "de-gendering" international human rights law to allow as much open-endedness as possible in the guarantee and safeguarding of individual liberties and rights, particularly when issues relating to sexual orientation and/or gender identity are involved. Asking whether human rights can exist without gender, however, means that we need to engage with the ongoing dilemma of whether, when resorting to human rights, we do so to emphasise the differences or the similarities of a given group with respect to the so-called majority. Joan Wallach Scott (2009) has aptly discussed this dilemma in her book *Only Paradoxes to Offer*, in which she has looked at the ways in which various French feminist writers sought to reconcile the need to articulate women's equality in relation to men with the need to point out the uniqueness of women's experiences.

When putting forward a vision of politics, as well as human rights, that has the ambition of being both emancipatory and egalitarian in its outlook, we are inevitably confronted with this paradox. When it comes to issues relating to sexual orientation and/or gender identity, more specifically, we are asked to reflect on whether LGBTQI persons should be protected under human rights by virtue of their inherent sameness with respect to the heterosexual, cisgender majority or whether their claims to rights arise out of, and are legitimised by, the uniqueness of their experiences, their narratives and the challenges they have encountered in life. The choice therefore appears to be between a liberal paradigm of human rights protection and one that is more emancipatory and radical in its premises and outcomes. Furthermore, in this context, both *gender-neutral* and *gender-specific* approaches to human rights can result in the exclusion of categories of individuals who may escape inclusion within the narrative of *sameness* or *difference*.

The recognition of the gendered nature of human rights therefore seems to be a guarantee for some and a constraint for others. Furthermore, tangential to the issue of the gendered nature of the law and human rights is also the question of the articulation of notions such as respectability, passing and coming out for LGBTQI persons. A *gender-neutral* paradigm of human rights could potentially shield those unwilling to publicly articulate their gender identity and/or sexual orientation. That means, for instance, that, under a *gender-neutral* human rights paradigm, trans individuals would not necessarily have to disclose their gender or the gender they were assigned at birth. At the same time, however, the enactment of a gender-neutral paradigm for human rights could also water down and partially delegitimise the specific struggles that a trans person may have encountered throughout life, thus denying the existence of the quite distinct obstacles and challenges that they face in society. At its very extreme, therefore, a gender-neutral paradigm could possibly deny the very existence of the conceptual category of "trans", thus undervaluing all specific struggles for the sake of principles of equality and universality.

Important for the purpose of this discussion is a reflection on what meanings the concept of gender possesses in light of contemporary human rights debates. Long confined to the realm of feminist and queer debates, the concept of "gender" has now become a ubiquitous term, popularised in the relatively recent advent of the so-called anti-gender movements (Kuhar 2014; Kováts 2016). More specifically, the word "gender" seems to recur in a vast array of insidious discourses concerning a disparate range of educational and civilisational values that are presumably jeopardised by two sets of arguments that have emerged in feminist and gender studies in the last few decades. These two sets of arguments concern, respectively, the idea that the concepts of masculinity and femininity may be socially constructed (Garbagnoli 2016, 189) and the discussion relating to the denaturalisation of the sexual order (Garbagnoli 2016, 189). This peculiar understanding of the term "gender" is indebted to the theological interventions of two popes – John Paul II and Benedict XVI (Guidi 2014; Garbagnoli 2016) – and is increasingly infiltrating popular educational and political discourses both across (Kuhar and Paternotte 2017; Kováts 2016) and outside Europe.[2]

In light of these developments, the concept of "gender" seems to have become the problematic receptacle of diverging configurations of what it means to have human rights as a (sexed and) gendered human being. "Anti-gender" campaigners in various countries, in particular, directly oppose achievements relating to both women (on reproduction, gender politics,

---

2 See the 7 November protest in São Paulo, Brazil, against philosopher Judith Butler, accused of threatening individuals' gender identity, as well as Brazilian values in general, because of her work in her famous book *Gender Trouble* (Butler 1990): see Jaschik (2017).

gender mainstreaming) and to LGBTQI persons (marriage equality) (Kováts 2016, 175). The concept of "gender ideology" becomes an "empty signifier", as Garbagnoli (2016, 201) has defined it, which can easily be adapted across national contexts, as well as can potentially cover a broad range of issues. What it effectively does is to frame discourses on rights in an antagonistic way, following the logic of "us vs them".

"Anti-gender movements", however, are not the only actors whose analytical focus insists on the meanings (and "dangers") of the concept of "gender". Under a different guise, the debate on the exclusion of trans women from the category of "womanhood", originating in the 1970s and made (in)famous by authors such as Janice Raymond (1979), has been transfigured into today's debates on the opposition between feminists who include trans women within their conceptions of "womanhood" and so-called trans-exclusionary radical feminists (TERFs). In particular, radical feminists categorised as TERFs substantially equate the concept of "womanhood" with biological determinism of the sexes (Hines 2017, 2), thus either denying or downplaying the experience and meaning of womanhood for trans women. Here, the concept of gender acquires an almost spatial significance, where the concept of what it means to be a "woman" possesses physical boundaries in need of protection from perceived incursions or challenges embodied by trans women.

Albeit incommensurable (and incomparable) as movements, what connects the phenomenon of "anti-gender movements" to the dispute between "trans-inclusionary" feminists and TERFs is an understanding of values as being configured as "antinomical", as Bobbio (1996) has argued. In particular, in his 1996 seminal book *The Age of Rights*, Bobbio proposed a problematic idea of the antinomical and heterogeneous character of values, whereby any concessions made to one group of individuals to their rights necessarily imply a loss of rights for a corresponding group of individuals. If read against the backdrop of the two phenomena we just illustrated – the rise of "anti-gender movements" and the debates on the inclusion/exclusion of trans women within feminist discourses – we can understand how human rights, seen through the prism of "gender", can be configured as a sort of "scarce resource" whose different patterns of allocation could favour specific groups of individuals to the detriment of others. This specific view could be fuelled by corollary considerations on who retains the monopoly on interpreting what it means to be a "woman" or what is the correct configuration of the relationship between the sexes and genders.

Bobbio's (1996) argument is relevant to understanding the conundrum we are facing when deciding between fostering a *gender-specific* paradigm of human rights vs a *gender-neutral* paradigm. It can be argued that much of this discussion, within the realm of human rights, can be articulated through the (specific) use of language, particularly if we adopt a structuralist perspective (O'Byrne 2012). Looking at the language of the law (and the interpretation thereof) can therefore help us to understand how gender is made sense of by legislative and juridical actors in line with sociological categories of action. In this regard, one interesting example relates to the linguistic practices enacted by the Commissioner for Human Rights of the Council of Europe on issues relating to sexual orientation and gender identity, complemented by observations pertaining to the case law of the ECommHR/ECtHR on the same issues.

Escaping the paradox between gender-specific rights and gender-neutral rights

In this section, I will focus on the usage of language in the case law of the ECommHR/ECtHR, but also predominantly in the work of the Commissioner for Human Rights, to illustrate the challenges – and possible solutions – to the paradox of uniqueness/sameness that I have previously outlined and potentially to the idea of the "antinomical" character of human rights. Overall, the linguistic practices of the ECtHR and of the Council of Europe are generally highly gendered. Whilst there is an increasing interest in notions relating to gender neutrality and issues such as intersexuality within the organisation, there is a very strong reproduction of binary gender categories at the institutional level. One observation to also include in this analysis is whether the "gendering" of human rights operated by the ECtHR, as well as by the Commissioner, participate in the articulation of a human rights paradigm in which the recognition of the rights of some individuals corresponds to the subtraction of rights from other groups.

This brief analysis is based on fieldwork undertaken in 2010 at the Office of former Commissioner for Human Rights Thomas Hammarberg, combined with some reflections on the relevant case law of the ECommHR/ECtHR. For the purpose of this discussion, however, the focus will be on the linguistic element (in relation to sexual orientation and gender identity) that characterises both the case law and the work of the (former) Commissioner. As far as the case law is concerned, since the first complaints in the 1950s relating to the criminalisation of same-sex sexual acts in the Federal German Republic,[3] the ECommHR/ECtHR has

---

3 See App. No. 104/55, *X v Federal Republic of Germany*, ECommHR, 17 December 1955; App. No. 167/56, *X v Federal Republic of Germany*, ECommHR, 28 September 1956; App. No. 530/59, *X v Federal Republic of Germany*, ECommHR, 4 January 1960; App. No. 5935/72, *X v. Federal Republic of Germany*, ECommHR, 30 September 1975.

fundamentally retained the same vocabulary concerning issues relating to sexuality and gender. On reflection, plaintiffs resorting to the ECommHR/ECtHR have fundamentally accepted – if not encouraged, as Johnson (2012, 33) argues – the circulation of an essentialist view of homosexuality. The extensive use in the case law of the ECommHR/ECtHR of the word *homosexual* is a paramount example of this. Notwithstanding attempts to free it from its original medical connotations, the word has substantially retained its pathologising aura. As such, it sheds a problematic light on the process whereby the individual is made a subject of human rights, as though "the homosexual" were a distinct anthropological character distinguished from "the straight plaintiff". Several cases heard by the ECommHR/ECtHR abundantly frame the plaintiff as the Foucauldian personage of the homosexual.[4]

The ECtHR, however, is not the only body at the Council of Europe concerned with choosing the vocabulary apt to describe sexual orientation and gender identity. I carried out this research during the preparation of the 2011 report on homophobia and transphobia in the 47 member states (Commissioner for Human Rights of the Council of Europe 2011); I came to realise that linguistic choices in the creation of this report were a fundamental component of the editing process.

Compared to the language deployed by the ECtHR, I found that, at the Office of the Commissioner, efforts were made to *de-essentialise* homosexuality. Where it was used in the report, the word *homosexual* was used as an adjective, rather than as a noun. The same applied to *lesbian* (a *lesbian* woman), as well as to *bisexual* (a *bisexual* person/man/woman) or *transgender* and *intersexual* (a *transgender*/*intersexual* person). Far from being superficial, the difference between *homosexual* (noun) and *homosexual* (adjective) acquires ontological relevance. *Homosexual* as a noun is self-sufficient and self-standing, and it may work to promote an essentialist conception of sexual orientation. Zwicky (in Livia and Hall 1997, 22) attributes the preference for adjectives rather than nouns to the fact that nouns reduce the individual to that single property, while adjectives designate one characteristic out of many. *Homosexual* (or *lesbian*, *bisexual* and so forth) as an adjective is therefore used as an *addition* – a non-essential part of the speech – not as a substitute for the individual themselves.

Another important aspect of linguistic choices enacted in the work of the Commissioner is that of favouring the use of the term *persons*

---

4 See App. No. 7525/76, *Dudgeon v United Kingdom*, ECtHR, 20 October 1981; App. No. 10581/83, *Norris v Ireland*, ECtHR, 26 October 1988; App. No. 15070/89, *Modinos v Cyprus*, ECtHR, 22 April 1993.

rather than *people* after adjectives such as *LGBT, gay, lesbian, bisexual, transgender* and *intersexual*. The *persons* vs *people* issue illustrates an important transition in conceptualisation: from an amorphous conglomeration of individuals to an organised and potentially empowered group. In line with the demands of liberal human rights rhetoric, the *persons* vs *people* issue signals the need to shift from an essentialist conception of sexual orientation and/or gender identity to a non-essentialist conception. While putting the individual at the forefront in all of her/his/their humanness, this endeavour simultaneously minimises the dimension of empowerment proper in the term *people*. The Commissioner's linguistics therefore have a problematic effect: downplaying the collective character of LGBTQI identities, while recasting individuals as relatively isolated from a socio-cultural community.

Compared with the ECtHR, the Office of the Commissioner has developed partly distinct linguistic practices. In fact, the Commissioner has almost entirely substituted the word *gay* for the word *homosexual*, with *gay* always used as an adjective (as in *gay man* or *gay men*). Zwicky (in Livia and Hall 1997, 22) illustrates this distinction by explaining the difference between *behaviour* and *identity*. In the case of the ECtHR, the *homosexual* is the taxonomic description of the medicalised homosexual, the Foucauldian *personage*. The Commissioner's choice to use *gay* rather than *homosexual* demonstrates an abandoning of taxonomic description. The word *gay* allows connection with fields of lived experience other than simply sexual desire or behaviour. In practice, it establishes a connection with relationships within the public sphere, with cultural phenomena, and with understandings and appropriations of homosexuality. Furthermore, in relation to the debate concerning the choice between *gender-specific* and *gender-neutral* human rights paradigms, this issue helps us to understand that a *gender-specific* paradigm may harbour a danger of essentialising the subjects of human rights as *solely* connoted by one unique characteristic (their sex or gender, sexual orientation, gender identity).

Linguistic differences between the ECtHR and the Commissioner, however, also vest in the sphere of trans rights. In particular, different uses of the terms *transgender* or *transsexual* (either as adjectives or nouns) can be observed. While the term *transgender* encompasses a wider range of individuals who cross gender lines in different ways, the term *transsexual* has a much stronger medical connotation and refers only to those who have undergone some form of gender reassignment procedure to cross the "line" of *sex*. All of the case law of the ECommHR/ECtHR to date has invariably adopted this "psychomedical construction" (Roen 2002, 502). Even in the landmark case of *Goodwin*,[5] the language employed is heavily connoted in medical terms. In considering the "applicant's situation as a transsexual" (*Goodwin*, at [76]), the ECtHR reinstates the importance of *passing* and, indirectly, of *respectability*. The ECtHR's approach here falls squarely within "liberal transsexual politics" (Roen 2002, 502), directly in opposition to the "radical politics of gender transgression" (Roen 2002, 502). Through the exclusive use of the noun *transsexual*, even when referring to trans people in general, the ECtHR thus contributes to the strong objectification of trans persons.

When it comes to gender identity, the Commissioner has adopted an approach that, contrarily to that of the ECommHR/ECtHR, is cautiously non-essentialist. In his 2011 report, the Commissioner questioned the requirement, in many Council of Europe member states, that an individual undergo gender reassignment – and complete sterilisation – to have their preferred name and/or gender recognised. Nonetheless, in the Commissioner's documents the emphasis remains on the crucial importance of an appropriate allocation of gender. The impression is that a substantial departure from the male/female binary has not happened in this context.

The non-essentialist approach to gender and gender identity endorsed by the Office of the Commissioner can also be said to be the product of close collaboration with the European transgender activist network, for example with the umbrella organisation Transgender Europe (TGEU). At the operational level, however, it is difficult for the actors involved to translate this commitment into an institutional report, such as that issued in 2011. A significant reason for this incomplete endorsement of a non-essentialist outlook on gender and gender identity derives from the difficulty in bringing together the requirements of the law and the disruptive potential of queer theory. In the work of the Commissioner, the *transgender* (person), while not treated as the medical *transsexual* portrayed by the ECommHR/ECtHR therefore remains partially embedded in the binary system of gender – a system highly functional to the workings of the law and the sole taxonomic language that the ECtHR understands and employs.

Conclusion: whose rights? Whose gender?

The discussion of both the case law of the ECommHR/ECtHR and the work of the Commissioner serve to illustrate the difficulties encountered

---

5 App. No. 28957/95, *Goodwin v United Kingdom*, ECtHR, 11 July 2002. In this case, the ECtHR had conceded that the "biological criteria" in the definition of the gender of the spouse had to be overcome, thus allowing transgender persons to marry someone of the opposite gender.

by various actors in the field of human rights when trying to grapple with issues relating to sexual orientation and gender identity that require, somehow, a broadening of categories such as "sexuality" or "gender". Indirectly, these issues also contribute to the debate on whether human rights should be gender-specific or gender-neutral. This is because, through processes of essentialisation, human rights run the risk of defining gay and/or trans human rights holders almost as a category discrete to (and separate from) straight and cisgender human rights holders.

The examples discussed in this brief analysis point in the direction of difficulty in dismantling the highly gendered nature of human rights in favour of a more flexible approach that recognises and gives legal dignity to the concept of "gender neutrality" or "gender plurality". At the same time, however, I hope that my discussion has also helped to illustrate how we cannot endlessly deconstruct human rights law by lapsing into a purely queer paradigm of fluidity. Such a choice would strongly call into question the usefulness and political power of identity politics as an instrument of political empowerment and a radical critique of extant institutions. The question of whether human rights can exist without gender can therefore be answered by saying that human rights should exist within the framework of an instrumental and pragmatic conception of gender, almost in the Rortian (1993) sense. This understanding of human rights should abandon the use of gender categories within the legal domain as a site of the reproduction of essentialised legal categories. Ultimately, human rights can coexist with a different conception of gender that includes notions of incoherence, non-linearity and incongruence in one's personal life and lived experiences.

References

Ammaturo, F.R. 2017. *European Sexual Citizenship: Human Rights, Bodies, and Identities*. Basingstoke: Palgrave.
Arendt, H. 2013. *The Human Condition*. Chicago, IL: University of Chicago Press.
Bobbio, N. 1996. *The Age of Rights*. Cambridge: Polity Press.
Butler, J. 1990. *Gender Trouble: Feminism and the Subversion of Identity*. New York: Routledge.
Commissioner for Human Rights of the Council of Europe. 2011. *Discrimination on Grounds of Sexual Orientation and Gender Identity*. Strasbourg: Council of Europe.
Dworkin, R. 1982. Law as Interpretation. *Critical Inquiry*, 9(1): 179–200.
Dworkin, R. 1986. *Law's Empire*. Cambridge, MA: Harvard University Press.

Fineman, M.A., Jackson, J.E., and Romero, A.P. (eds). 2009. *Feminist and Queer Legal Theory: Intimate Encounters, Uncomfortable Conversations.* London: Routledge.

Garbagnoli, S. 2016. Against the Heresy of Immanence: Vatican's "Gender" as a New Rhetorical Device against the Denaturalisation of the Sexual Order. *Religion and Gender*, 6(2): 187–204.

Guidi, L. 2014. Il Genere: Un Campo di Battaglia. *La Camera Blu: Rivista di Studi di Genere*, 10, online at www.serena.unina.it/index.php/camerablu/article/view/2588

Hines, S. 2017. The Feminist Frontier: On Trans and Feminism. *Journal of Gender Studies*, 18 December, online at www.tandfonline.com/doi/abs/10.1080/095892 36.2017.1411791

Jaschik, S. 2017. Judith Butler on Being Attacked in Brazil. *Inside Higher Ed*, 13 November, online at www.insidehighered.com/news/2017/11/13/judith-butler-discusses-being-burned-effigy-and-protested-brazil

Johnson, P. 2012. *Homosexuality and the European Court of Human Rights.* London: Routledge.

Kováts, E. 2016. *The Emergence of Powerful Anti-Gender Movements in Europe and the Crisis of Liberal Democracy.* In M. Köttig, R. Bitzan and A. Petö (eds). 2016. *Gender and Far Right Politics in Europe*, pp. 175–189. Basingstoke: Palgrave.

Kuhar, R. 2014. Playing with Science: Sexual Citizenship and the Roman Catholic Church Counternarratives in Slovenia and Croatia. *Women's Studies International Forum*, 49: 84–92.

Kuhar, R., and Paternotte, D. 2017. *Anti-Gender Campaigns in Europe: Mobilising against Equality.* London: Rowman & Littlefield International.

Livia, A., and Hall, K. (eds). 1997. *Queerly Phrased: Language, Gender and Sexuality.* New York: Oxford University Press.

Moran, L. 1996. *The Homosexuality of the Law.* London: Routledge.

O'Byrne, D. 2012. On the Sociology of Human Rights: Theorising the Language-Structure of Rights. *Sociology*, 46(5): 829–843.

Raymond, J.G. 1979. *The Transsexual Empire: The Making of the She-Male.* Boston, MA: Beacon Press.

Roen, K. 2002. "Either/Or" and "Both/Neither": Discursive Tensions in Transgender Politics. *Signs*, 27(2): 501–522.

Rorty, R. 1993. *Human Rights, Rationality and Sentimentality.* In A.S. Rathore and A. Cistelecan (eds). 1993. *Wronging Rights? Philosophical Challenges for Human Rights*, pp. 1–34. London: Routledge.

Scott, J.W. 2009. *Only Paradoxes to Offer: French Feminists and the Rights of Man.* Cambridge, MA: Harvard University Press.

Valdes, F. 1997. Beyond Sexual Orientation in Queer Legal Theory: Majoritarianism, Multidimensionality, and Responsibility in Social Justice Scholarship or Legal Scholars as Cultural Warriors. *Denver University Law Review*, 74: 1409–1464.

Warner, M. (ed.). 1993. *Fear of a Queer Planet: Queer Politics and Social Theory.* Minneapolis, MN: University of Minnesota Press.

Case law

App. No. 104/55, *X v Federal Republic of Germany*, ECommHR, 17 December 1955.

App. No. 167/56, *X v Federal Republic of Germany*, ECommHR, 28 September 1956.

App. No. 530/59, *X v Federal Republic of Germany*, ECommHR, 4 January 1960.

App. No. 5935/72, *X v. Federal Republic of Germany*, ECommHR, 30 September 1975.

App. No. 7525/76, *Dudgeon v United Kingdom*, ECtHR, 20 October 1981.

App. No. 10581/83, *Norris v Ireland*, ECtHR, 26 October 1988.

App. No. 15070/89, *Modinos v Cyprus*, ECtHR, 22 April 1993.

App. No. 28957/95, *Goodwin v United Kingdom*, ECtHR, 11 July 2002.

4 Linguistic traps

Identity and differences through institutions

Carlotta Cossutta

The relationship between gender and institutions has been problematic since the beginning, because institutions themselves are the first to have contributed, often decisively, to the production and reproduction of sexism. In particular, institutions have acted in two ways: through discrimination of some groups – from women to homosexuals, transsexuals, intersex, etc. – highlighting their peculiarities; or in the opposite direction, by making the same groups invisible through the use of a neutral universal.

I want to focus primarily on the language of institutions, starting from the case of the Italian language, in which gender is very obvious, because of the gendered articles and the absence of a neutral pronoun. I will use, in particular, the *Raccomandazioni per un uso non sessista della lingua italiana* [Recommendations for a non-sexist use of the Italian language] contained in *Il sessismo nella lingua italiana* [*Sexism in the Italian Language*], written by Alma Sabatini and Marcella Mariana (1987) for the Presidency of the Council of Ministers and the National Commission for Equality and Equal Opportunities between Men and Women in 1986 to understand how institutions have struggled with this issue (Sabatini and Mariana 1987). This document is particularly relevant in the Italian context because it is the first (and only, at the national level) to specifically address the language of the institutions, promoting a language that neither privileges the male gender nor perpetuates a series of prejudices against women, thus respecting both genders.

Sabatini and Mariana show clearly how Italian is a gendered language with a male dominancy. As Nicoletta Marini-Maio (2016, 6) points out, "psychological research has demonstrated that gender-exclusive language is often deliberate and may involve gender discriminatory intentions and attitudes". It is also true that users are not fully in control of their language choices in matters of gender because linguistic habits are strongly tied to certain behaviours that become socially prevalent and cue language patterns.

In other words, what is behind the use of the masculine gender as a gender-neutral marker is maleness affirmed as a habit and social norm within a heteronormative framework.

The language, in this sense, is a symptom and a result of social structures, not a neutral tool. Thus every social change could lead to a change in the language, but what happens when that change comes from the institutions? Could the language be changed by law?

Based on this reflection, I would like to examine the case of intersex[1] infants and the laws that allow for the assignment of a third sex at birth. In particular, I will take into account the German law of 2013 recognising intersexuality as a third sex category.[2] Germany is the first member of the European Union to legally recognise the possibility of registration as intersex, but the law was the subject of criticism, especially from intersex activists. I will relate this criticism to some of the criticism that similar laws in Australia and New Zealand have received, to show how the critics share the idea that this legal recognition of intersex provides only a new category without addressing the discrimination that intersex people face or the binary system that produces this discrimination.

I will position the intersex case within the framework of language to problematise the relationship between institutional choices and social change. The underlying key question, then, may be summed up in this way: what does it mean to introduce a new sex without the corresponding language to name it, to talk about it? How can we introduce a third sex into a binary gendered language? The risk here is of (re)producing new oppressions on the basis of the linguistic structures that shape our conception of the world, outside the sphere of laws.

Moreover, we might ask, to what extent do institutions influence the promotion and protection of differences? What is the relationship between these choices and social changes and movements? And to what extent do

---

1 There is a current debate about the terminology. Most of the medical professions, many intersex parents, and some intersex activists and associations have agreed to replace the terms *intersex* and *intersexuality* with the new *disturbs of sexual development* (DSD) to avoid conflating matters of anatomic/gonadic/chromosomal sex with sexual preference or gender identity, and to refer to the most recent specific medical classification of the intersex conditions. However, other intersex activists and associations, as well as some scholars, academics and medical professionals, prefer to keep using the terms *intersex* and *intersexuality* because they believe that DSD incorrectly suggests intersex to be always and only a pathological condition. For them, the terminology *disturbs of sexual development* implies illness, abnormality and deviance, and it represents and ratifies a pathologisation of intersex persons. I choose to use the term *intersex* to avoid the pure medical dimension.

2 Gesetz zur Änderung personenstandsrechtlicher Vorschriften (Personenstandsrechts-Änderungsgesetz, or PStRÄndG).

they capture a promotion that has already taken place thanks to the social movements that produce changes at other levels?

Premises

Alma Sabatini was a feminist linguist who, in 1986, on the recommendation of the National Equal Opportunities Commission of the Presidency of the Council of Ministers, wrote a text aiming to offer guidelines to mitigate the sexism within the Italian language. Following an investigation into the terminology used in textbooks and the mass media, Sabatini emphasised the prevalence of the male gender – used in Italian with double valence (the so-called neutral masculine) – that eliminates the female subject from speeches. She stressed the lack of institutional terms, as well as power declined to women (*ministra, assessora, sindaca*) and the prestige granted to a male term, but not to the female counterpart.

Sabatini affirms: "The theoretical premise underlying this work is that language not only reflects the society that speaks it, but also influences and limits its thinking, imagination and social and cultural development" (Sabatini and Mariana 1987, 18).

Sabatini's fundamental reflections, and her recommendations, have highlighted the absence of women from the public scene, but at the same time they have shown how criticising the masculine universal does not mean stepping out of gender binarism. The structure of the Italian language, in fact, requires a constant explication of the gender to which one belongs, coming to attribute it even to inanimate things. As Charlotte Ross (2017) points out:

> Tables, chairs, trains, boats and planes have genders. Moreover, the gendering of many nouns is deeply sexist. The default sex if the sex is unknown is male: i.e. rather than just speaking about a baby, people refer to "un bimbo" [a baby boy]; when asking if someone has siblings, often the questioner enquires about "fratelli" [brothers].

Furthermore, to express this gender affiliation, it is possible in Italian to refer only to the masculine or to the feminine, since there is no neutral gender that can be used.

Over the last few years, many social movements that define themselves as queer have tried to question this imposed binarism through the use of the asterisk, *, or the "at" symbol, @, as a sign to replace the gendered word ending. In this sense, the movements speak of *queerizzare* ("queering") the Italian language. This means thinking of the way in which the language can be reimagined from within so as to oppose, following the indications of queer linguistics,[3] essentialist, naturalised and hegemonic ideas about gender and sexuality. These experiments, however, do not find acceptance in the institutional spheres, in which they are still perceived as elements of disorder (Baldo 2017; Marotta and Monaco 2016).

In the tradition of Italian feminism since the late 1960s, the relationship of theory with the law has always been problematic and has been questioned in many ways. Starting from the reflection of Milan's Feminist Bookstore Collective *Non credere di avere dei diritti* [*Don't You Believe You Have Any Rights*] (Libreria delle donne di Milano 1987), the inclusion of women in the current legal system was considered a risk. In this text on justice and law, some theses were supported: law is conceivable only as translatable and the source of social existence; justice can go beyond the law through the formulation of political judgment on injustice; doing justice means practising, each in the place in which it is, an idea of the right world based primarily on the enhancement of experience and the plot of human relationships.

As Tamar Pitch (2004, 62) points out:

> [A] common feature of the feminist approach is the questioning of the positive definition of law, and of the more rigid tradition of juridical positivism, producing norms and thinking on norms outside the perimeter of the statute law, sometimes confronting the issues of so-called legal pluralism, sometimes attacking it. In much feminism, moreover, as practice and thought, law and justice, law and morality are not only not easily separable, but jealously held together. This not only because feminism constitutes "external point of view", for this same source of criticism of law in the name of values, but because it reasons on the norms in view of the possible production of just rules.

Feminist critics of the law questioned the idea of the neutrality of the law, theorising that the legal system is always the result of the structures of power in society. When the law takes into account sexuality and gender roles, it reproduces the patriarchal structure of the world and it changes only if social movements modify the power relations.

For this reason, I choose to adopt a feminist stance from which to analyse the exclusion and inclusion criteria that the law proposes, starting from gender. I will do so starting from the case of intersex people and the laws that have emerged in the last few years to allow them to be registered outside

---

3 Queer linguistics is a definition given by Heiko Motschenbacher (2011) to that branch of linguistics which, inspired by theorisations on the queer, critically analyses essentialist, hegemonic and naturalised notions about gender and sexuality.

of the "male" and "female" categories. To analyse these laws, however, I choose to use the words of people who fight for intersex rights, before mine, so that I can use the *privilege* of a public space to give voice to those too often ignored. Furthermore, to counteract the alleged objectivity of the law, I believe that lived experience is one of the most valid starting points for rethinking justice. Finally, the words of people involved in social movements can challenge the law, and the academic debate, pointing out the distance between their examples and the results that emerge in the legal and institutional system.

Intersex and law

The relationship between the categories of the law, also expressed, in the Italian case, by a gendered language, and the differences of bodies and subjectivities becomes very stringent in the case of those who do not adhere perfectly to the gender norm.[4] The laws depict a supposed universal *homo juridicus*, but, as Alexander Schuster (2011, 21) points out, "racism and sexism have shown that this *homo juridicus* was not representing any and every human being, but took the appearance of the masculine side of humanity. Moreover, his skin had a very specific colour: white." We can add that this *homo juridicus* is also heterosexual and cisgender. Thanks to the struggles of women, lesbian, gay, bisexual and transgender (LGBT) people, and allies, however, the law has had to adapt and recognise sexual differences. In recent years, however, these differences have become especially relevant with regard to anti-discrimination laws and attention has shifted from sex to gender, from biological to social distinctions. The development of the concept of gender was very useful in pointing out the social nature of the sexual differences (Scott 1986) and the institutions became more aware of the role they can play in social change, which can affect discrimination and oppression based on gender. It became clear that the reasons for discriminating were not chromosomes and biological traits per se, but rather the social constructs of "man" and "woman", and that is why the attention of the institutions shifted from sex to gender. For this very reason, reference to "sex" in public policies and legal discourse faded out in favour of "gender", so that expressions such as "gender equality", "gender balancing", "gender neutrality" are now in common usage.

---

4 As Carol Smart (1989, 4) argues in her ground-breaking book *Feminism and the Power of Law*, legal norms and assumptions play a powerful role in asserting how things are, "impos[ing their] definition of events on everyday life", in part because law represents itself as embodying "a claim to a superior and official field of knowledge".

The legal system participates in this terminological change, to which the notion of gender identity offers a significant contribution. As Schuster (2011, 28) points out:

> [W]ith the shift from sex to gender the cryptotype of a sexual dualism as a social construct comes to the surface. By embracing the term gender jurists show aware-ness of the fact that rules are in reality linked to the social role assigned either to men or to women.

This shift to gender, however, seems only cosmetic if we think about intersex – about infants who are reduced to female or male following medical protocols through surgery and reassignment of sex (Greenberg 2012). The legal definition of sex, in fact, is built on its naturalistic evidence, without questioning the biological and medical assumptions that there are only two sexes. This image of sex makes it a category, a label for classifying individuals, and a requisite to which consequences are attached, not least of which is inequality.

According to the UN Office of the High Commissioner for Human Rights, intersex people are born with sex characteristics (including genitals, gonads and chromosome patterns) that do not fit typical binary notions of male or female bodies. *Intersex* is an umbrella term used to describe a wide range of natural bodily variations. In some cases, intersex traits are visible at birth; in others, they do not become apparent until puberty. Some chromosomal intersex variations may not be physically apparent at all. Some intersex traits are not always visible at birth: some babies may be born with ambiguous genitals, while others may have ambiguous internal organs (testes and ovaries). Other people will not become aware that they are intersex unless they receive genetic testing, because it does not manifest in their phenotype. People whose characteristics are neither typically "all male" or typically "all female" at birth are intersex.[5]

Beginning in the 1950s, the standard protocol for treating new-born babies with ambiguous genitalia involved surgical alteration of "unacceptable" genitalia into "normal" genitalia. Although surgeries to "create a definite sex" have now diminished, doctors still frequently perform cosmetic genital surgeries to conform a child's genitalia to a binary sex norm. Surgeons necessarily perform cosmetic genital surgeries on intersex

---

5 In biological terms, sex may be determined by a number of factors present at birth, including: the number and type of sex chromosomes; the type of gonads (ovaries or testicles); the sex hormones; the internal reproductive anatomy (such as the uterus in females); and the external genitalia.

children without their own consent, because this operation takes place in the first months of life, but with the consent of parents who believe the operation to be necessary and efficacious. These surgeries aim to create a penis or a vagina that matches the heterosexual binary model: the penis should be long enough to penetrate a vagina and a vagina should be deep enough to be penetrated. Endocrinologists have manipulated patients' hormones to try to get the bodies of patients to do what they thought was necessary not only for physical health, but for psycho-social health (that is, to get the body to look sexually "normal").

If the intersex movement[6] is successful at stopping cosmetic genital surgeries on infants born with an intersex condition, when these children reach adulthood, they may be confronted with the same legal problems that confront transgender people: state control over the determination of their legal sex. Institution sex determination actions could arise in two scenarios: people with sex attributes that are not clearly male or female may have their legal sex challenged by the state or other individuals; and people with an intersex condition may seek to change the sex indicated on their legal documents because it does not comport with their own gender identity. Both of these scenarios may lead to state intervention.

Until sex reassignment surgery became available in the latter part of the twentieth century, legal institutions were rarely asked to determine whether a person qualified as a man or a woman. Although people with an intersex condition appear in ancient Greek mythology, early religious tracts and English writings from the sixteenth century, legal institutions did not begin to wrestle seriously with this issue until the 1970s. This is relevant because it shows how the law started to take into account the intersex condition only after an intersex rights movement arises, while *hermaphrodites* had previously been only a *mostrum* or treated following medical protocols. In this way, the legal institutions regulated the intersex condition only because they faced social change.

Significantly, in 2013 in Germany, a law to introduce a third sex was approved. German parents of "intersex" children are able to register the baby in such a way that they could avoid choosing between female and male. Alongside the categories of "M" and "F" a new category, "X", was introduced. However, the German government and legal experts are keen to stress that this third blank box is not an official third gender, or an "other" box, so it does not mean that there are now three recognised genders in Germany; rather, it is seen as a temporary solution for very specific intersex cases – and only for intersex people. Moreover, these children are not

---

6 See Chase (2006).

expected to live their lives as "X"s, but to make a decision to be either male or female at a non-specified point in the future.

This law was approved in a particular context: in Germany, there have recently been changes in the laws that regulate gender identity. Germany now allows a person to change their legal gender if they can prove both a medical diagnosis of transsexualism and if they have been living as their preferred sex for a minimum of three years. The previous laws were far stricter: transgender people had to prove themselves permanently infertile and sterilised, as well as were forced to have gender reassignment surgery to change any external sexual characteristics to a "significant approximation" of the desired sex. This change was the result of a trans rights movement and testifies to the German Parliament's interest in regulating sex and sexuality in such a way as to open up the possibility for different people to be recognised under law.

The law on the "third sex" has given rise to numerous criticisms, especially of the decision to mark this third possibility with an "X", to signify a blank space as though intersex were an empty space, *something lacking*. Hoping to create another official identification beyond male or female, such as "inter" or "diverse", Dritte Option [Third Option], a network of groups that claims intersex rights, brought a case to the German Constitutional Court. The German Ethics Council had recommended in 2012 that the government have an "other" category. The X, the blank space, is problematic because it introduces a new category without naming it and hence indicates an expectation that this registration will not be permanent.

In August 2016, the German High Court rejected the creation of a third gender category of "inter" to describe people born with a reproductive or sexual anatomy that does not fit the typical definitions of female or male. A woman had requested a respective modification of their birth certificate at the registry office in Gehrden, in July 2014. The request was forwarded to the district court in Hannover, which rejected the application. The woman and the advocacy group submitted a complaint to the appellate court in Celle, which also rejected it. Consequently, the complainants took their case to the Federal Court of Justice, the highest appellate court in Germany for civil and criminal cases. The Court rejected the complaint on 22 June 2016.[7] The person now identifies as "intersex" and submitted a genetic analysis showing that they were neither man nor woman. The panel nonetheless ruled that German law would not allow the entry of a third option of "inter" or "diverse" in the birth certificate and saw no reason to

7 The court ruling is online at http://dritte-option.de/wp-content/uploads/2016/08/anonymisierter-BGH-Beschluss-1.pdf

refer the matter to the German Constitutional Court. The High Court said that it found no violation of the plaintiff's basic rights since intersexual people had been able, since 2013, to leave the gender entry in German birth certificates blank – yet this case illustrates how this option limits the self-determination of intersex people.

As Zwischengeschlecht (2013, emphasis original), an intersex rights group, points out:

> The new German birth certificate law is *not* about making an optional "3rd gender entry" available for the intersexed, but in fact *prohibits "ambiguous" children to be registered as "M" or "F"*. Therefore, for the persons concerned, this new law is stigmatising, bound to result in more mutilating "genital corrections", and generally *bad news* – quite contrary to the "uplifting" "gender progress" fantasy the media made out of it, *at the expense of even more mutilated children*, again.

Organization Intersex International Europe (OII Europe 2013) also denounces the decision:

> [I]nstead of leaving sex registration open for all, and not just intersex children, once again special rules are created, which produce exclusions. The living conditions of the vast majority of intersex people will not improve as a result. What we need is an end to the externally determined gender assignment, the practice of sexed standardization and mutilation, as well as medical authority of definition on sex.

These criticisms show that the possibility of being included in a third category other than male and female is discriminatory because it is offered only to intersex people, but above all it does not solve the very material problem of neonatal surgical operations carried out to adapt an infant's gender to the norm. Furthermore, the same associations underline how the rules that supervise surgical operations do not depend on the law, but on medical protocols that are considered purely technical. The medical protocols, in fact, are produced in the medical associations and are presented as the result of a scientific decision that is claimed to be neutral. Yet many scholars, starting from Foucault, have shown, conversely, how biology and medicine are, like laws, the result of power relations and social structures, and that these change across time and place. Donna Haraway (2003, 2) criticises this presumed objectivity, affirming that:

> [B]iology is restlessly historical, all the way down. There is no border where evolution ends and history begins, where genes stop and

environment takes up, where culture rules and nature submits, or vice versa. Instead there are turtles all the way down.

She proposes a neologism that could represent this intersection of biology and cultural processes: the idea of *naturculture*, which represents exactly the entangled bond between nature and culture.

OII Europe (2013) asks:

> Who determines that a child "can be assigned to neither the female nor the male sex"? According to current practice: only medicine. The power to define what sex is and who is assigned to which gender remains intact with the new regulation.

And the power to define what is female and what is male still depends on supposed natural laws.

It is possible to compare the German law with a similar law in New Zealand, which allows passports to feature an "X" sex descriptor. These were originally introduced for transgender people in transition, but certificates are now available on registration of birth showing "indeterminate" sex if it is not possible to assign a sex to the new-born infant. Specifically, the New Zealand Department of Internal Affairs states that a person's sex can be recorded as indeterminate at the time of birth if it cannot be ascertained that the person is either male or female and there are a number of people who have been so recorded.

In Australia, the Australian Health Data Dictionary (AIHW 2012) portrays *sex* as including "male", "female" and "intersex or indeterminate", as well as "not stated/inadequately described". There are two different codes that can be used to register the sex of a new-born baby. The first, CODE 3, states that *intersex* or *indeterminate*:

> . . . is normally used for babies for whom sex has not been determined for whatever reason. Should not generally be used on data collection forms completed by the respondent. Should only be used if the person or respondent volunteers that the person is intersex or where it otherwise becomes clear during the collection process that the individual is neither male nor female.

The second, CODE 9, indicates that *Not stated/inadequately described* "is not to be used on primary collection forms. It is primarily for use in administrative collections when transferring data from data sets where the item has not been collected" (AIHW 2012).

In both New Zealand and Australia, therefore, we can see the same legal choice as was posed in Germany: to create a new category that allows (or constrains) intersex people to be registered without using the male or female boxes. In this case, however, as Carpenter (2013) points out:

> [T]he availability of blank or indeterminate sex assignments at birth has no ameliorating impact on surgical interventions. Indeed, [New Zealand] may be an outlier in the region, with hastier decision-making. This is not surprising: the problem these laws seek to define and manage is the physical body of intersex infants.

Once again, the law, although producing new categories, does not seem to affect the material processes that lead to reassignment of intersex infants to the male or female sex because it does not take into account the medical protocols. In this sense, the abstraction of the law emerges strongly. It can certainly have a symbolic impact on society (even if this, in the case of German law, is criticised), but it fails to intervene in medical power because it does not directly address it (for example by prohibiting reassignment operations on infants). Moreover, doctors possess knowledge and skills that are said to be vital to the health of intersex children, and so if parents were to refuse medical intervention, they may be said to be endangering their children's lives. Thus medical power is a bio-political power (Foucault 2008) that overcomes the law, often in the name of "natural" biological laws.

These natural laws, however, are constantly reproduced by social norm. As the report of the Third Intersex Forum, held in Malta in 2013, asserts:

> We support gender diversity, however, we believe that in most of today's environments, children would be challenged by not being identified as boys or girls. Thus we recommend that intersex children be registered as females or males with the awareness that, like all people, they may grow up to identify as a different sex or gender. We reject normalising medical treatments on children.
>
> Sex or gender classifications should be changeable non-bureaucratically on request by the individual. Adults and capable minors should be enabled to choose between F, M, non-binary, or multiple options.
>
> All people regardless of their identities have the right to full equality and participation in society.
>
> In the future, as with race or religion, sex or gender should not be a category on birth certificates or identification documents for anybody.
>
> (Third Intersex Forum 2013)

And as Morgan Holmes (2004) points out:

> [M]uch of the existing work on cultural systems that incorporate a "third sex" portray[s] simplistic visions in which societies with more than two sex/gender categories are cast as superior to those that divide the world into just two. [. . . R]*ecognition* of third sexes and third genders is not equal to *valuing* the presence of those who were neither male nor female, and often hinges on the explicit devaluation of women.

Once again, in this perspective, the "third sex" in a new category that is simply added to the binary, without subverting it.

In this sense, one part of the intersex movement involves asking for the removal of sex and gender, like race and religion, from official documentation entirely, even if, as Morgan Carpenter (2016) argues, this is "a more universal, long-term policy goal". This policy is seen not only as a way of avoiding segregating the intersex people within the "third sex", but also as a way of affecting sexual binarism itself, even in the medical sphere. It is, then, not only a struggle to reform the laws, but also a struggle that aims to change the very heart of the legal system – the binary categorization. In this sense, the biological studies of Anne Fausto-Sterling (1993, 2000) are particularly interesting, claiming that there are more than two sexes – or, rather, that sex is a *spectrum* of differentiations and not a binary system. If we think of sexual difference as a *spectrum*, it is not only hard to imagine a categorisation, but also it is a challenge to the medical knowledge that can affect the medical protocols applied to, and hence the lives of, people.

Anna Grear (2011, 49) offers an alternative to both the sex dichotomy and the rigidity of a third sex, noting that:

> [I]t seems more just to characterise the universal subject of law not as sexually differentiated in a dichotomous sense but as sexually variegated and mutable. One way of doing this is to see sex (and potentially gender) not as a binary but as existing on an embodied multi-sexed/ omnigendered spectrum (or continuum) that moves between notional spectrum-extremes of "male" and "female" but, crucially, without essentialising them. This spectrum, thoroughly embodied, could embrace a related proliferation of sexual and gender identities and also explicitly allow space for self-ascribed and transgender (and transsexual) identifications.

The removal of sex from documents can open the way towards a more radical chance of self-determination for all. As other intersex activists point out:

We share [with the transgender community] the issue of self-determination: the right of the individual to choose. . . . Those of us whose bodies cannot be easily categorized into the either/or binary system automatically transgress this code of silence. The heterosexist, dualistic system is built on a shaky foundation of lies and half truths. [. . .] It is based upon a lie: that in the natural world, each person is born either male or female.

(Nevada and Chase 1995, 11)

This claim shows how the law, which constantly reproduces the binary system even when adding a third exception, is based on a *lie*: on the idea that there are only two sexes, naturally and clearly divided.

The abolition of the legal category "sex", instead, would mean that the legal comparison between men and women would be impossible – a comparison that is vital for sexual equality rights. New instruments of legal protection against discrimination and inequality would thus have to be developed. The abolition of sex categories would have the liberating effect of ending the ontologisation and essentialisation of differences between the sexes, and would demonstrate that the current hegemonic two-sex model is open to change.[8]

Moreover, the criticisms of the "third sex" laws that I have presented in this chapter illustrate that: "Sex matters. It matters socially, politically, and legally. Most important, it matters to the people who are harmed by society's failure to protect them from discriminatory practices based on sex stereotypes" (Greenberg 2012, 135).

Conclusions

As Sabatini's work has shown, language, like law and institutions, expresses the social structure within which it is determined and, in the case of sex and gender, constantly reproduces gender binarism, as well as the male and heterosexual domination on which patriarchy is based. In this chapter,

---

8 Angela Kolbe (2009, 163), however, points out that there are also some risks to the abolition of the legal category of sex: "[I]ndeed, a complete abolition does not seem to be appropriate now. Discrimination and sexual hierarchies still exist and would become unnamable if we were to eliminate 'sex' from the law. As long as these problems remain, mechanisms of protection like anti-discrimination-norms are necessary. But one alternative may already be possible: to do away with the categories 'female' and 'male' while keeping the category 'sex'. A broad interpretation of this term would be necessary. [. . . A] broader definition of 'sex' would embrace not only the common sexes male and female but also intersexual, androgyne and a good deal more."

I have retraced the criticisms that intersex activists have raised to the German law introducing a "third sex", and of the similar laws in Australia and New Zealand, to highlight how the introduction of new categories does not undermine this binarism. The choice of the German legislators to identify the "third sex" with an "X" – with an empty space – also signals the absence of a language (legal or not) able to give space to the differences without transforming them into exceptions that confirm the binary standard. Introducing new categories, but keeping the legal system unchanged, therefore means producing new opportunities for discrimination rather than spaces for freedom and self-definition.

However, the attention to language on which this chapter is based and the lived experiences of activists involved in social movements allow us to imagine different outcomes. In fact, language changes as societies change, thanks to the active and transformative intervention of the speakers, who introduce new linguistic forms into use and promote their spread to the extent that they become new rules. In the same way, for example, the proposal of many intersex activists to abolish the identification of sex from documents would allow the opening of spaces for the transformation of institutions and laws without proposing new categories, and without positioning those categories in opposition to society. Certainly, this proposal itself contains many risks including, as emphasized by Kolbe (2009), that of limiting the ability of the law to combat discrimination and therefore limiting the instruments available for the protection of minorities.[9] But the proposal to remove sex from official registers, such as of birth, also contains the risk of reaffirming a neutral universal, which will remain heterosexual and male if the gendered power relations in the society do not change. In this sense, this proposal also signals a utopia capable of finding forms of self-regulation and self-government – and this is a challenge that intersex activists, starting from their bodies too often subjected to institutional oppression and mutilation, seem ready to grasp.

References

Australian Institute of Health and Welfare (AIHW) (2012) *National Health Data Dictionary*, Canberra: AIHW.

9 Although Devina Cooper and Flora Renz (2016, 488) suggest that, "without certifying individual gender at birth, state law can continue to recognize gender, and regulate the gendered decisions, practices, and resource allocations of other organizational bodies in various ways. This becomes apparent when we consider other areas of inequality and identity, such as religion and sexuality."

Baldo, M. (2017) Frocie, femminelle, terrone, polentone e favolosità varie. Quando il queer è di casa. *Queer Italia Network*, 13 May, online at www.queeritalia.com/blog/2017/5/13/frocie-femminelle-terrone-polentone-e-favolosit-varie-quando-il-queer-di-casa1

Carpenter, M. (2013) Open birth sex assignments do not reduce surgical interventions. *Intersex Human Rights Australia*, 4 November, online at https://ihra.org.au/24097/flexible-or-open-birth-sex-assignments-have-no-impact-on-surgical-interventions/

Carpenter, M. (2016) The human rights of intersex people: addressing harmful practices and rhetoric of change. *Reproductive Health Matters*, 24(47): 74–84.

Chase, C (2006) Hermaphrodites with an attitude: mapping the emergence of intersex political activism. In S. Stryker and S. Whittle (eds), *The Transgender Studies Reader*, New York: Routledge, pp. 300–314.

Cooper, D., and Renz, F. (2016) If the state decertified gender, what might happen to its meaning and value? *Journal of Law and Society*, 43(4): 483–505.

Fausto-Sterling, A. (1993) The five sexes. *The Sciences*, 33(2): 20–24.

Fausto-Sterling, A. (2000) The five sexes, revisited. *The Sciences*, 40(4): 18–23.

Foucault, M. (2008) *The Birth of Biopolitics: Lectures at the Collège de France, 1978–1979*, New York: Springer.

Grear, A. (2011) Sexing the matrix: embodiment, disembodiment and the law—towards the re-gendering of legal rationality. In J. Jones, A. Grear, R.A. Fenton and K. Stevenson (eds), *Gender Sexualities and Law*, New York and London: Routledge, pp. 39–52.

Greenberg, J.A. (2012) *Intersexuality and the Law: Why Sex Matters*, New York: New York University Press.

Haraway, D. (2003) Introduction: a kinship of feminist figurations. In *The Haraway Reader*, New York and London: Routledge, pp. 1–6.

Holmes, M. (2004) Locating third sexes. *Transformations Journal*, 8, online at www.transformationsjournal.org/wp-content/uploads/2017/01/Holmes_Transformations08.pdf

Kolbe, A. (2009) Intersex: a blank space in German law? In M. Holmes (ed.), *Critical Intersex*, Farnham: Ashgate, pp. 147–170.

Libreria delle donne di Milano (1987) *Non credere di avere dei diritti*, Turin: Rosenberg & Sellier.

Marini-Maio, N. (2016) It's not only a matter of pronouns. *Gender/Sexuality/Italy*, 28 December, online at www.gendersexualityitaly.com/its-not-only-a-matter-of-pronouns/

Marotta, I., and Monaco, S. (2016) Un linguaggio più inclusivo? Rischi e asterischi nella lingua italiana. *Gender/Sexuality/Italy*, 27 December, online at www.gendersexualityitaly.com/4-un-linguaggio-piu-inclusivo-rischi-e-asterischi-nella-lingua-italiana/

Motschenbacher, H. (2011) Taking queer linguistics further: sociolinguistics and critical heteronormativity research. *International Journal of the Sociology of Language*, 212: 149–179.

Organisation Intersex International Europe (OII Europe) (2013) Sham package for intersex: leaving sex entry open is not an option, 15 February, online at https://oiieurope.org/bluff-package-for-inter-leaving-sex-entry-open-is-not-an-option/

Pitch, T. (2004) *I diritti fondamentali: differenze culturali, disuguaglianze sociali, differenza sessuale*, Torino: Giappichelli.

Ross, C. (2017) Qu@*ring the Italian language. *Queer Italia Network*, 12 January, online at www.queeritalia.com/blog/2017/1/10/quring-the-italian-language

Sabatini, A., and Mariana, M. (1987) *Il sessismo nella lingua italiana*, Rome: Presidenza del Consiglio dei Ministri, Direzione generale delle informazioni della editoria e della proprietà letteraria, artistica e scientifica.

Schuster, A. (2001) Gender and beyond: disaggregating legal categories. In *Equality and Justice: Sexual Orientation and Gender Identity in the XXI Century*, Udine: Forum, pp. 21–40.

Scott, J. (1986) Gender: a useful category of historical analysis. *American Historical Review*, 91(5) 1053–1075.

Smart, C. (1989) *Feminism and the Power of Law*, London: Routledge.

Third Intersex Forum (2013) *Public Statement by the Third International Intersex Forum*, 1 December, online at https://ihra.org.au/24241/public-statement-by-the-third-international-intersex-forum/

Zwischengeschlecht (2013) "Intersex: third gender in Germany" (Spiegel, Huff Post, Guardian, . . .): silly season fantasies vs reality of genital mutilations. *STOP Intersex Genital Mutilations in Children's Clinics*, 1 November, online at http://stop.genitalmutilation.org/post/Intersex-3rd-gender-in-Germany-Silly-season-fantasies-vs-reality-of-genital-mutilations

5 Subjectivity, gender and agency

Petr Agha

The relationship between discourse, sex, and the body has attracted sustained interest from scholars in sociology and cultural studies over decades now. It is only quite recently, however, that sociological analyses of sexuality have begun to explore the specificity of the body and its relationship to human agency. This chapter suggests that, far from serving as a passive surface upon which sexual scripts are inscribed, the body in sexual action is itself a dynamic force in generating sexual subjectivities. This is related to the way in which the praxeological aspects of sex are always corporeal and that corporeality is indivisibly related to individual agency. The specific configuration of sexual practices is central to the making of sexual identities. Indeed, it is through such a configuration that the sexual subject is brought into being. Yet human agency is a central feature of the process, rendering it a project that develops over time. It can be too easy to dismiss the internet and its fast-moving trends as frivolous and representative of some great cultural decline. But for those who do not see themselves represented in traditional forms of media or social institutions, there are online spaces in which certain social technologies and languages can work to supplement this gap. Inspired by my own immersion and development in these spaces, I want to legitimize the contemporary, online iterations of nonbinary transgender communities through theoretical analysis. My contribution to the theories and analyses surrounding transgender lives and experiences is indebted to the groundbreaking work of previous and current trans scholars, activists, and writers, as well as their allies. Although the field from which this work has grown has sprouted in many different directions, it is vital to recall that certain central tenets to the beginnings of trans (sometimes intersected with queer) theory and trans studies provide a context that shapes and supports my exploration into online nonbinary subjectivity formation. This field is considered recent, but the theorists involved in the formation often weave other works and narratives from across human history to avoid naturalizing the idea that trans people and the promotion of their voices are an entirely new phenomenon. There have always been people who live and flourish outside of the coercive gender binary that has come to structure so many social and cultural contexts, but I believe that the particular discursive characteristics within online cultures that allow the mobilization of "nonbinary" as an umbrella term have unprecedentedly generative capabilities.

The individual stories presented in this chapter connect to debates in transgendered communities and to the more general project of exploring the broader analytic agendas of the thesis. Personal stories provide constructed accounts of how particular individuals pursue their own construction of identity through fields of knowledgeability. The limited repertoire of representations and stories means that certain unintelligible experiences, events, and identities will not be accommodated easily within the range of available cultural, public, and institutional narratives. The narratives of transgender people provide a site in which to explore issues associated with embodiment, identities, poststructuralist and essentialist/modernist theories, and conceptualizations of persons. Attention to these particular narratives and forms of embodiment allows us to explore existing theories—and to set up an analysis of sex and gender through its embodied, physical, state and institutional forms.

This chapter is based on a series of semi-structured interviews with individual trans people whose personal experiences with institutions are diverse, as are their opinions of the social situation of trans individuals in the Czech Republic. Czech trans people are therefore situated within a discourse that is firmly grounded in the concept of sexual identity and binary gender differentiation. The prevalent discourse is dominated by a medical definition of trans people as distinct from certain norms and, as such, is defined as a disorder that needs to be rectified, according to a standard that is found in normative medical and expert texts. The legal framework reflects medical normativity; the concept of gender identity is unknown, and it explicitly uses the term "sex change." The change of biological sex, as understood by the Czech laws, is *de facto* a process of reconciliation between the internal gender identity and sexual identity as understood by the law. The views articulated by the participants in this study are testament to the fact that trans people's opinions on the same core issues can diverge vastly: we have not been able to establish any universal "trans experience" even in our relatively small sample, although normative texts often assume that such exists. However, the members of the Czech trans community who took part in the research repeatedly mentioned as problematic the tendency of the Czech medical establishment to prescribe individuals' transition options in rigid terms, and they critiqued the Czech legal system for incorporating mandatory sterilization, limited naming conventions, gatekeeping by doctors and regulatory bodies, and the obligation to dissolve a marriage or a civil union upon gender recognition.

To understand their situation and how Czech society frames gender identities, we will first briefly visit the history of the Czech trans community, although there are very little hard data or academic texts to which to refer, pre-1989—and what are completely missing are the accounts of the members of the community themselves. A lot of emphasis in this part of the chapter is put on how the medical discourse was being shaped after 1940. The (lack of) evolution of the perception of trans people is perhaps best captured by referring to the most dominant and influential narrative that shapes the available identities from which trans people can choose. Another powerful discourse, which, hand in hand with the medical one, co-creates the world for trans people, is the law. Czech law does not draw information on the lives of trans people from consistent engagement with the trans community, but rather relies completely on the deep-seated convictions of medical professionals who perpetuate the transsexual label. As a result of this, the Czech law lays down several institutions and procedures that trans people wishing to transition cannot escape—perhaps most tellingly demonstrated by the requirements of sterilization and divorce. Both the medical and the legal discourse present their understanding of trans people as based on self-evident facts—referring, of course, to the binary understating of human existence—and not on communication with the trans community wishing to transition. The procedure is almost fully covered by public health insurance and, without the consent of the state bodies, there can be no transition; hence those trans people who start the procedure and wish to complete it must always conform to the pre-existing categories and understanding. Our research shows, however, that trans people perceive their identities, bodies, and sexuality in a significant variety of ways, and that their perceptions differ from the official medical discourse. In this part of the chapter, we confront the official narrative, expressed in the language of the law, with the actual responses of real trans people. The chapter concludes with observations and comments.

Fragments of Czech trans history

The leading representative (before the fall of communism) of the sexologists' discourse was Professor Josef Hynie (1974, p. 73), who defined transsexuality as "the innermost feeling and conviction of belonging to the other sex on the basis of another differentiation of the brain and disposition." The Czech Institute of Sexology, which caters to transsexual patients, first records a diagnosis of transsexuality in 1942. Until the late 1960s, there were no more than a couple such patients a year. In the 1970s and the 1980s, the numbers of persons diagnosed as transsexual still remained in single digits (Weiss, Fifkova, and Procházka 2008, p. 19). The first of what the Czech discourse on transgender issues calls "sex confirmation surgeries" seems to have taken place in the mid-1960s (Working Group for the Issues of Sexual Minorities 2007, p. 28). Transsexuality was seen as a medical-psychological problem of an "inborn" "discordance" between the "biological and psychological" (Haderka 1986, p. 213). This can be illustrated, for example, by the fact that an internal instruction issued by the Czech Ministry of Health on doctors' recommendations for name changes prescribed as a condition that the individual must conform to the gender-appropriate behavior of their new "sex" (Ministry of Health of the Czech Republic 1979). Postoperative transsexual persons had to have a "sufficiently persuasive appearance as a person of the opposite sex." Their "reproductive function" was mandatorily "disabled"—in other words, they were sterilized. In the context of Czech medical discourse, attempts are made to approach the trans body and trans physicality as something that needs to be "rectified," reinstated into the binary categories of man/woman and approximate to the normative ideal. In addition to hormone therapy, trans people who enter into the process of transformation undergo, in the case of female-to-male (FtM), chest surgery (mastectomy), and removal of the ovaries and uterus (hysterectomy); in the case of male-to-female (MtF), the removal of the testicles and penis (orchiectomy and penectomy), and the formation of a vagina (vaginoplasty). Penis reconstruction is considered a "superstructure," and the decision is left to the trans person (Ministry of Health of the Czech Republic 1979). As noted earlier, in the Czech medical discourse, the functioning of the organs is considered to be an important criterion. However, Professor Hynie did not recommend genital surgery because plastic surgeons, at that time, were not able to create sensitive and functional genitals. The criterion of organ function and full sex life was considered the most important. Since plastic surgery is not able to create a fully functional and sensitive penis, doctors will consider the wishes of the individual trans person when deciding whether or not to undertake penile reconstruction, especially because such reconstruction does not always achieve the desired results and is often associated with postoperative complications. When sex confirmation surgery became available in the 1980s, it was dealt with under the rubric of "treatment of serious sexual disorders," together with operations on intersex individuals ("hermaphrodites") and "deviants," such as sadists, pedophiles, etc. (Ministry of Health of the Czech Republic 1970).[1]

---

1   The view of transsexuality as a "sexual deviation" was also repeatedly mentioned in medical texts: see Jahodová (2011).

As can be seen from Jan Raboch's (1984, p. 97) medical sexology scripts published in the 1980s, only those trans people who were "mentally stable" and "socially well-adapted" were able to undergo sex change and live in in the majority society. The central concern was no longer the functionality of sexual organs, but the psychic stability and social adaptability of trans people. In this period and then in the early 1990s, in medical texts or in interviews with doctors we come across the concept of transsexuality understood as sexual deviation. Raboch (1984, pp. 96–97) himself directly defines transsexuality as a "sexual deviation, in which an individual uniquely developed male or female has an urgent consciousness of belonging to the opposite sex." This attitude persists even today, as before 1989, with transsexuality positioned in opposition to the sexual norm of heterosexuality and identification with male or female roles in accordance with the anatomical structure of the body.

Since the 1960s, there has been a slight shift in the discourse, despite the fact that the fundamentals have remained unchanged. Attempts to measure trans people's bodily dimensions to determine their "suitability" for transition were gradually abandoned. Additionally, the concept of transsexuality as a brain disorder shifted to signify instead a long-term unchanging identification with the "opposite" gender from that assigned at birth (Dvořáčková 2008) Other techniques of "measuring" transsexuality, such as the plethysmograph, which attempted to gauge the supposed arousal of trans people while being shown erotic footage featuring different sexualities as a "proof" of their trans identity, have also gradually fallen out of favor as a mainstream practice. The number of people seeking medical transition increased sharply after 1989. Multiple factors contributed to the rising numbers of transition-related surgeries performed, one being the gradual lifting of taboos around sexuality-related topics, along with a growing adherence to the ideals of authenticity and autonomy in society. Information on transsexuality, the healthcare options in the Czech medical system, and the experiences of some trans people began to be featured in newspapers and popular magazines. Changes to the diagnostic practices of doctors and the shortening of the expected minimal length of the transition process from five-and-a-half years to three years (Fifková 2008) also affected the viability of medical transition. The original schema had trans people undergo various physical and psychological examinations in the first year, begin hormone replacement therapy (HRT) in the second year, acquire the doctor's recommendation for a name change to neutral in the third year, and only then be able to set an appointment with the regulatory body approving transition-related surgeries. A name change to an explicitly gendered one in accordance with the person's identified gender was possible only in the fifth year, after the individual underwent sterilization surgery (Fifková 2008).

The field of medicine has largely defined the norms framing discussions of trans subjectivity. Although the trans subject, as understood today, did not appear until the defining of the term "transsexual," medical professionals within the field of sexology in the late nineteenth and early twentieth centuries discussed "sexual inversion" as an innate reversal of gender habits, dress, mannerisms, and desires. The cases presented by sexologists of patients with sexual inversion reflected the medical professional's observations of the patient's body, as well as narratives of their life experiences. These cases played a fundamental role in forming the medical origin story of the trans subject. In the accounts given to sexologists, patients often conveyed that they felt their biological body was standing in the way of their being the sex they felt themselves to be. Medical professionals positioned these accounts as "problems" and began to investigate cures for those who were sexual inverts. Most thought that if medicine could realign the body with the mind, the patient would no longer express signs of sexual deviancy. This discourse from patients and sexologists constructed the medicalized narrative of inversion, which then becomes the medical narrative of transsexual subjectivity. The trans subject produced by medicine was recognizable, but only through the repetition of a specific narrative of being born in the wrong body. This "born in the wrong body" narrative has since become one of the dominant origin stories of trans subjectivity.

"True sex": the law and confirmation of one's sex

According to the dominant account of trans subjectivity, the body is inherently malleable and should be changed to align with the nonmalleable innate gender identity of the mind. These changes occur most often through medical interventions such as HRT and various surgeries to create a desired sexed body and gendered appearance. Understanding the body to be malleable allows the trans person to understand the body as a tool to be manipulated, with the end result reflecting an inner self. The Czech medical literature operates exclusively with the term "transsexuality," which is reflected in the legal discourse as well. Czech sexologists address the presence of trans people as gender disorder and pathology. Probably because of this pathologization of transsexuality and the idea that a hormonal, and especially an operative, solution can cure and normalize the "patient," the procedure has, since its inception, been fully paid for under public health insurance. The Czech law operates on the following three assumptions, which, taken together and each separately, continue to normatively ensure the biological (reproductive) binary of men and women.

1   The heteronormative character of the law manifests itself in the requirement that a marriage be dissolved before a person can submit to sex
confirmation surgery.[2]

2   The biological attachment to "sex" is apparent in the requirement of
surgical intervention for any legal recognition of a person's preferred
sex. The law recognizes the possibility that "biological sex" and "psychological sex" are misaligned, and it enables their "realignment,"
medically and legally. What it does not recognize is the possibility that
gender identity can be different from biological sex without a person
wishing to physically modify their body, including their sex characteristics. The law does not accept that it might be called to recognize such
a situation and to enable some legal recognition of a person's preferred
gender or to allow for a name change without that person first having
submitted to gender confirmation surgery.

3   The law is incapable of transcending the male/female binary, perhaps
best demonstrated in the so-called real life test, which required a person
to demonstrate the "proven ability to live in the opposite sex role." This
test is required preceding sex reassignment surgery (together with other
requirements, at which we look next). This proves to medical professionals that the person has made a complete transformation and is ready
for permanent surgery, and that the person is ready to pass as one of the
two available sexes.

What the Czech law currently calls "sex reassignment" is now regulated by
the 2012 Act on Specific Health Services.[3] This piece of legislation marks
the latest development in the story of trans people living in the Czech
Republic. The first explicit legal provision addressing the legal recognition of sex change appeared in 1991, in the Act on Popular Health Care.[4]
The legal recognition of preferred sex (in birth records) was long opposed
by the medical establishment.[5] It was eventually made possible in 1980,
but only through an internal instruction issued by the Czech Ministry of
Health, which does not have a character of a legal instrument and was
thus not legally binding (Ministry of Health of the Czech Republic 1979).
The instruction provided guidelines for recommendations to the registry

2 Or, as the new Civil Code stipulates in a subsidiary way, in cases in which the marriage has
not been dissolved, the marriage ceases to exist *ex lege.*

3 Act No. 373/2011 Coll., on Specific Health Services.

4 Act No. 20/1966 Coll., on Popular Health Care, as amended by 548/1991.

5 The Final Resolution from a medical symposium, which took place in 1969 in Bouzov,
concluded that "it is impossible, from a medicinal and natural science perspective, to accept
that an operation can change a person's sex".

offices to amend records where a person had submitted to sex confirmation surgery. Changing one's name and birth records (with an *ex nunc* effect) was possible under the general legal provisions and informally addressed through the non-binding instruction. The mid-1980s were also the time when limited legal issues relating to transsexuality started to be discussed by legal scholars.

Section 27a(1) of the 1991 Act on Popular Health Care stipulated that:

> [C]astrations, stereotactical operations and surgeries for transsexuals are only performed based on request by the person on which they are to be performed, and only after approval from an expert committee, which shall consist of a lawyer, at least two medical specialists in the relevant area, and two other doctors which will not carry out the medical treatment.

The particulars of the surgical treatment were not legally specified. The rules relating to surgery were complemented by the legally guaranteed possibility of a name change in 2000.[6]

The 2012 Act on Specific Health Services is more detailed in its definition of what constitutes sex confirmation surgery than was previously the case. For example, it makes the "disabling of the reproductive function"—meaning sterilization—an integral part of the procedure. While it was previously the practice of authorities to require proof of sterility for the purposes of changes in birth records, the statute has now made this a legal requirement. A further legal specification came into force on 1 January 2014 via the new Czech Civil Code. Unlike the previous Civil Code, which was silent on the issue,[7] the new Civil Code explicitly addresses "sex change."[8] It stipulates, in section 29(1), that that the "sex change" occurs "through surgery with the simultaneous disabling of the reproductive function and the transformation of sexual organs." Any medical attention given during the supposed six phases of transition[9] is paid for by public health insurance (Raichlová and Procházka 2002, p. 110). Those who seek to transition are required to contribute only to the costs of HRT and to pay for "cosmetic treatment," which includes epilation, breast augmentation, the insertion of prosthetic testes,[10] voice therapy, and thyroid eminence elimination.

---

6 Act No. 301/2000 Coll., on Register Offices, Name and Surname.
7 Act No. 40/1964 Coll., Civil Code.
8 Act No. 89/2012 Coll., Civil Code.
9 Referred to as the six stages of "sex change," as identified by Czech sexologists, comprising (1) diagnostics, (2) decision making, (3) the real-life test and real life experience, (4) hormonal therapy, (5) operation, and (6) the postoperative stage: see Fifková (2008).
10 Fifková (2008, p. 110).

Section 21(1) of the 2012 Act on Specific Health Services defines surgical intervention (termed "sex change") in the following terms:

> The term sex change in transsexual patients is to mean the medical operations, whose aim is to change sex operatively with the *concurrent disabling of the reproductive function.* A transsexual patient is a person who is affected by a *permanent discordance* between psychological and physical sex ("sexual identification disorder").

Aside from the diagnostic requirement and mandatory sterility, the Act also requires a "real-life test" and civil status conditions for surgery:

> Surgical operations leading to a sex change can be performed on persons a) in whom the sexual identity disorder has been definitively diagnosed and who *have proven the ability to permanently live as a person of the opposite sex,* and b) who have *never been married or entered into registered partnership* (or a foreign equivalent), or prove that their marriage or registered partnership has *ended.*[11]

In addition to a written request from the transgender person, the surgical procedure requires the approval of an expert panel.[12] The panel is established by the Ministry of Health and consists of a medical professional employed by the Ministry, a sexologist, a psychiatrist, a clinical psychologist, an expert of diabetology[13] and endocrinology, an obstetrician-gynaecologist, and a lawyer with medical law expertise.[14] These experts must not be employed by the healthcare provider and must not be the doctor directly treating the "patient." The transgender person is invited to meetings of the panel;[15] their personal doctor might be invited to join the panel's meeting. The doctor is not to be present during the panel's interview of the transgender person.[16] After deliberation, the panel adopts a position. A positive position, recommending surgical intervention, requires the consent of all panel members.[17] The positive position of the expert panel is one of the documents, alongside the request of the "patient,"[18] on the basis of which the healthcare provider then proceeds to

---

11 Act No. 373/2011 Coll., on Specific Health Services, s. 21(2).
12 Act No. 373/2011 Coll., on Specific Health Services, s. 21(3)(a) and (b).
13 That is, the study of the diagnosis and treatment of diabetes.
14 Act No. 373/2011 Coll., on Specific Health Services, s. 22(1).
15 Act No. 373/2011 Coll., on Specific Health Services, s. 22(4).
16 Act No. 373/2011 Coll., on Specific Health Services, s. 22(7).
17 Act No. 373/2011 Coll., on Specific Health Services, s. 22(6).
18 Or that of the legal guardian.

surgery.[19] The expert panel does not appear to be an administrative body nor is its decision an administrative decision. As a consequence, it does not seem to be possible to appeal—and, indeed, the 2012 Act on Specific Health Services certainly does not foresee that possibility. Between 2012 and 2014, 173 applications were registered, and all but one were accepted. This system produces a situation in which trans people are presupposed to want surgery and, as our research shows, a large number of them do so. Hormone therapy is only a part of the process; a trans person has one option only and that is to undergo sex confirmation surgery.

The legal procedure to obtain recognition of one's preferred sex consists of an amendment to the birth records and the issuance of a new birth number.[20] The change is recorded on the basis of a written confirmation by the healthcare provider about the surgical intervention (termed the "sex change"). The Act on Register Offices prohibits a man from changing his name to a woman's name and vice versa.[21] In the Czech language, most first names, as well as surnames,[22] easily identify a person as male or female. There are, however, names and surnames that are neutral, and the Act enables persons who transition to use a neutral name, on the basis of their request and a certificate from the healthcare provider, where the person is being treated.[23]

There are three problems with this process. The first is that anecdotal evidence suggests that the willingness of the individual registrars to perform the change and to accept the chosen neutral name varies (Fifková 2008, p. 197).

The second problem is that the change is entirely dependent on the assessment of the doctor. While "undergoing sex change" can be interpreted extensively to include HRT, it seems to exclude transgender people who have no desire to eventually undergo surgery, but have a gender identity not corresponding to their birth-assigned sex. Even more so, it excludes transgender people who do not seek treatment at all.

Third, the Act explicitly states that a "change of name will not be allowed if a person assigned male at birth requests a change to a female first name and vice versa."[24] It is not entirely clear whether, after surgery, a transgender

---

19 Act No. 373/2011 Coll., on Specific Health Services, s. 21(3). In the case of persons with diminished capacity, the consent of a court is also required. In that case, the healthcare provider applies to a court to attain consent with the surgery: Act No. 373/2011 Coll., on Specific Health Services, s. 22(10).

20 Act No. 133/2000 Coll., on Register Offices, s. 17(2)(d).

21 Act No. 133/2000 Coll., on Register Offices, s. 72(3).

22 Most commonly, the suffix *ová* is added to a man's surname.

23 Act No. 301/2000 Coll., on Register Offices, Name and Surname, s. 72(5).

24 Act No. 301/2000 Coll., on Register Offices, Name and Surname, s. 72 (3).

person can change from a neutral name to a name that corresponds to their newly recognized legal sex/gender. These decisions would, however, be at the full discretion of the register office, and a change would not have to be performed as a matter of right.[25]

Following sex confirmation surgery, a person is considered, by law, to have their newly recognized "sex." Those who have undergone sex/gender confirmation surgery are not barred from entering into a marriage or a registered partnership. They are not legally barred from becoming a parent, but the requirement of "disabling of the reproductive function" contained in the Civil Code[26] means, in practice, that they will not be able to become biological parents.

The voices of trans people: gender, sex, subjectivity

The research that forms the backbone of this chapter, conducted in late 2016, departed from the focus on the medicalization of gender identity and expert discourse that has been prevalent in the Czech society, to look instead at how transgender individuals shape their (own) social identities. Because the research comprises a relatively small sample of 17 semi-structured interviews, it cannot be taken as an exhaustive portrait of Czech trans people; however, its qualitative nature enables us to portray the Czech trans community—to a limited degree, of course. It tells the story of 17 diverse individuals struggling in a society that has ready-made identities for everyone into which they cannot fit.

Before we move on with the descriptive part of the text, let us issue a little caveat, which explains the particulars of the Czech situation. The trans community is a part of the wider lesbian, gay, bisexual, and transgender (LGBT) movement, although it is much smaller and is quite fragmented. The lines of fragmentation are characterized along the lines indicated earlier in this chapter. In a nutshell, there are different generations of trans people whose views differ significantly, as do their self-perceptions and identification. This split reflects their relation to the LGBT community as such, and it also means that there are significant difference in the types of policy that they do or do not advocate. Therefore, not only are there individual preferences and desires at play, but also, from a wider perspective, it could be said that there are roughly two groups of trans individuals, only one of which is active in

---

25 In Act No. 301/2000 Coll., on Register Offices, Name and Surname, s. 72(5), the change is mandated by the Act.
26 Act No. 89/2012 Coll., Civil Code, s. 29(1). The requirement of sterilization has always been part of the operative procedure, even though it was legally codified only recently.

the public space, lobbying and advocating for change. This group, according to our research, identifies with labels such as "transgender," while the other one perceives itself as "transsexual." The goals of those active in trans advocacy are very similar to those of their European counterparts, because the Czech discourse is one of the least friendly discourses in Europe. There is no consistent data collection on trans-related issues; what is available mostly comprises segments from more general LGBT surveys or (shadow) reports by human rights agencies.

It is alleged (although there are no hard data to support this) that trans people make up some 0.10 percent of the Czech population—that is, around 1,000 people. The focus of this survey was on trans people as a broad category that is subject to various kinds of marginalization. There are no precise statistical data on the number of people who undergo what is, in the Czech discourse, called "sex change" surgery. Today, around 50 people undergo this operation each year, but this number takes into account older trans people taking advantage of the current more favorable situation in medicine and society. Broadly speaking, we can identify two groups when it comes to how trans people tend to identify within the existing discourse in the Czech context. One group is characterized by a tendency towards gender essentialism. Members of this group were generally more likely to identify with the label *transsexual*. Most emphasized the unchangeable quality of their own gender identity;[27] some were suspicious of gender theory as a potential "threat" to the essentialist medical discourse that, in their view, rightly legitimizes fixed binary genders, including those of trans people who follow the expected transition path and identify in binary terms. They appear less keen to be involved in discourses perceived as "activist," and, on the whole, showed a lower degree of criticism of the current medical practices and codes of conduct, or expressed concerns that criticisms of it would jeopardize the funding of transition as part of public health care.

The second group of participants conceptualized their identity as more of a human rights issue. They tended not to share a single identity label such as *transsexual*, but used a wider variety of descriptors in their interviews, including *transgender*, *queer*, and *genderqueer*, or otherwise displayed some degree of nonbinary self-identification. Most, but not all, had been designated female at birth; their ages varied from early 20s to 40s.

---

27 To clarify, there is no issue when an individual trans person asserts that their identity is unchangeable and strictly binary. What is problematic is the assumption that this is the *only* way to exist as trans in society, which has so far been the prevailing assumption in the medical and legal discourses in the Czech Republic, contributing to the pathologization of trans identities and the coercive nature of gender recognition procedures.

We shall now take a closer look at the issues that trans people identified in their interviews as the most pressing concerns in their lives.

Naming conventions

Naming conventions are currently based on birth-assigned gender, which makes trans people particularly noticeable for, for example, having a different appearance from what is socially expected on the basis of their assigned name.[28] Since names are defined as "feminine" and "masculine" in the law, and it is expressly prohibited for individuals categorized as male to have "feminine" names and vice versa, trans people are immediately "outed" by their legal names prior to name change and/or gender recognition. Czech law now allows a person to change their name to an explicitly gender-neutral one even without undergoing sterilization.

Unlike most of the other areas of inquiry, there was a virtually unanimous consensus that linguistically enforcing gender neutrality on *all* trans people by default was detrimental. Among the group that did not have significant problems with medical transition requirements as such (group one), the only common criticisms were that a woman (or a man) should be named clearly and that imposing a gender-neutral name was an infringement on their right to identify as they saw fit. Among the more "activist" group (group two), the focus was on the human rights aspect of prescribing particular naming practices to trans people and on the impossibility of choosing a gender-neutral name without negotiating systemic coercion around naming:

> No, [I wouldn't take] a neutral name after gender recognition. I'm not even sure what my name is right now. I picked a name, argued with the lady registering them, then she let me have it. But I'm certainly not going to change my name fifty times, because that's counterproductive.
>
> (David)

Compulsory sterilization

The sterilization requirement was often brought up by participants who had considered starting a family using their reproductive function.

---

28 Czech naming conventions are rigorously and explicitly policed in laws, such as the Name Register Act, not only in relation to trans people, but also in the legal definition of "feminine surnames" as derived from and secondary to their base forms (termed "masculine"), or in the demand to provide independent linguistic reviews for names that are considered not to exist in Czech. There is thus a clear imperative expressed by such laws to render society linguistically homogeneous and easily categorizable along perceived gender lines.

In the interviews, contrary to the sexological discourse, there was not a universal rejection of the idea of giving birth among participants designated female at birth; one person had done so in the past before being sterilized, and another would have considered it if sterilization had not been the only way of obtaining gender recognition. In fact, the participants felt that they or others around them were being deprived of a choice that they should have had a right to make:

> The other operation [hysterectomy] was really only because of my documents. Now I'm sorry I did it, in a way. For instance we're trying for a baby, my wife hasn't been able to get pregnant. I'm just thinking: you know, if only I had these organs, I might have been able to have the baby myself and now I can't, because I don't have them. And you know, it's kind of unfair that you shouldn't be allowed to reproduce.
>
> (Roman)

There was a strong consciousness of the arbitrariness of this requirement and of the fact that it personally limited their life choices, both in the context of health and more broadly:

> And this [new] nationwide committee [. . .] is so that the Czech Republic can say why there are so many people undergoing sterilization and castration every year. Because we have the highest number in the [European Union], so all the people who see the committee and have the surgery, they're the ones who are voluntary. So the Czech Republic can say that all these numbers, these are voluntary sterilizations, castrations, which isn't entirely true. We're not doing them voluntarily, we're doing them because there's no other choice. But on the surface, it looks voluntary.
>
> (Roman)

> Sterilization should definitely not be necessary, or tied to some legislation – it should be voluntarily done on request. Castration applies here too, sterilization, castration. As for modifying the genitals, definitely not, don't touch. For the state to decide what I have between my legs, they have to be insane. [. . .] No, definitely not, definite no to sterilization, no to forced sex modification. All that has to be on request. If someone wants these things, that's fine. If someone doesn't, don't make them. Don't make them.
>
> (David)

Many participants highlighted the link between sterilization as a means to gender recognition and the role it played in their (coerced) decision to undergo sterilization surgery. Two of the participants who had undergone sterilization specifically remarked that it was done primarily, if not only, for the sake of gender recognition and that if their documentation, along with the attendant discrimination, had not been at stake, they would not have opted to be sterilized:

> The only thing I can say I delayed for two years, I delayed sterilization, and I felt a bit of pressure [from the doctor] as if I should want it, because what am I going to use these organs for, I'll have better facial hair afterwards, these are some of the things he said. And he probably took it as some expression of manhood, or an expression that I really wanted to be the opposite gender, or I felt it as this pressure to prove, by having this surgery, that I really want to transition and to finish it. Another surgery [aside from sterilization] wasn't necessary by him, but the pressure was there and it's a fact that after those two years I realized just how hard it was in many ways with the [identity] documents I had. So I had the [sterilization] surgery. But it was more for this reason, not because I would intrinsically feel I wanted these organs gone. [. . .]
>
> No. I wouldn't have it [sterilization surgery] done. Maybe if I had health problems, as they say, but that is again only if. I still have a vagina anyway, something [health-related] could still happen to that, but I definitely wouldn't do it voluntarily.
>
> (Roman)

> It's total nonsense to legally prescribe that I have to have a hysterectomy, because that will make me a man. It's totally bogus, it's not going to change my chromosomal makeup, it is just nonsense of the highest order. Unfortunately it's dictated to us. [...] I won't get the [correct] documents otherwise. It's not voluntary, I didn't feel I needed to have a hysterectomy, it went against my feelings, I don't agree with it.
>
> (David)

These examples demonstrate that the definition of "voluntary" does not sit easily with these silently occurring scenarios of trans people consciously opting for sterilization because it is the only way in which they can achieve legal recognition. Participants who articulated criticisms of sterilization in general were also critical of the way in which it is currently carried out administratively in the Czech Republic, with individuals having to "pass" before a regulatory committee:

To me, the committee is useless, of course. I think it would be enough, if you're going [to a specialist] somewhere who assists you and knows what you're like and what you want, then why not make it possible that way. Why do you have to face some committee – it seems pointless to me and kind of degrading. To answer these people you barely know all these things they ask, sometimes pretty intimate. Why do you have to go through it all, it's completely pointless.

(Roman)

I'm not happy with the fact that the committee is sometimes useless. In a way, it's really degrading. […] I don't see why strangers should decide what I want or not.

(Patrik)

Conclusions: trans identities in perspective

The research has shown that, despite the widely standardized sexological narrative of "true transsexuality" or "typical transition," there is a great variety articulated by Czech trans people. Where criticism appears in the interview sample, it is most commonly aimed at the three pillars of the current standard for medical and legal transition in the Czech Republic: naming conventions, compulsory sterilization, and the dissolution of marriage or a civil union as a prerequisite of gender recognition. A common problem thematized in the interviews was the medical establishment's drive to strictly categorize each trans person, both in terms of gender as male or female and in terms of sexuality as purely gay/lesbian or heterosexual, leading many to strategically choose the expected answers so as to be able to access transition.

More than 60 percent of respondents pointed towards the fact that trans people should be given the space in which to articulate their identity on their own terms, without being made to fit categories that they would not personally use for self-description. About 50 percent were of the opinion that any treatments, including HRT and/or transition surgeries, should remain recognized as medically necessary for those trans people who wish to undergo them, rather than compulsory. Choosing to undergo one treatment (such as HRT) should, however, not be taken as automatic consent to other treatment (such as surgery), unless desired by the individual.

Generally speaking, trans people are more reliant on healthcare services than lesbian, gay, or bisexual people. Like any cisgender person, they do engage with healthcare professionals for routine reasons (such as standard checkups and routine medical care) and in relation to acute or chronic illness/conditions. It is common for trans people who are questioning their gender identity, are unsure of their feelings, or are experiencing mental distress to seek a psychologist or psychiatrist in the first instance. For this reason, psychologists' and psychiatrists' familiarity with trans issues is paramount, along with the ability to react appropriately to the trans person's needs, including a referral to a sexologist, if desirable:

> In the beginning I just went to a regular psychiatrist who didn't specialize in this in any way, and I was really lucky because this was back when I still had no idea myself. So I went there saying I was depressed and so on. And I mentioned this [gender identity] towards the very end of the session, when "they" was already shaking my hand goodbye. [...] I had no idea what to expect, if [the psychiatrist] was going to send me to a mental hospital or what. But "they" acted amazing in that "they" instantly gave me the contact details for [the sexologist] and told me what to do. "They" were the first who started treating me like I wanted. So that was really great.
>
> (Jindra)

> I had a psychiatrist who already knew back then [before the participant decided to transition], I still see [the psychiatrist] now. [T]hen [before the participant decided] It was actually "them" who told me to seek this kind of help and asked around "their" colleagues and "they" recommended me to see the sexologist.
>
> (Lucie)

For those trans people who do not wish to align with the medical definition of transsexuality, yet wish to obtain any of the transition-related body modifications, the situation becomes precarious. Even those doctors who accept transgender, genderqueer, and nonbinary identities find themselves unable to refer the individuals for surgery because it will not be covered under public health insurance without the committee's stamp of approval.

Another common trend highlighted in the interviews was the attempt to fit the trans person into a rigid framework of categories related both to gender and to sexuality. The interviews suggest that the aim of the consultations has been less to understand each individual trans person's identity, and more to fit their gender and sexuality into predetermined categories. One of the participants summarizes the general attitude thus:

> To many of [the psychologist's] questions I just answered, after he asked is this black or white, I said grey. No. It's either black or white, so just choose. That really annoyed me, and after that I started answering with what he wanted to hear, just so he could tick off each box as "yes" or "no."
>
> (Jindra)

One other problem that emerges from the interviews is that, when seeking gender reassignment (through hormones and surgery), trans people are diagnosed with and treated for gender dysphoria. This is viewed as problematic for many trans people, who see their being trans as a social variation. Many of our respondents also felt that practitioners asserted narrow definitions and restricted understandings of gender with an expectation that clients would conform to these. Here, the problem lay in that they identified as neither male nor female, so struggled to fit within (and conform to) this gender framework. Diagnostic references listing trans as an identity disorder comprise a categorization with which many trans people feel uncomfortable, because for them there is no problem with their identity, but rather with the categorization and constraints imposed on them by others. It was also evident in our data that trans people felt that many of the questions they were asked and/or physical examinations that were undertaken in clinical settings were unnecessarily intrusive. While there may be legitimate reasons for particular questions or tests, practitioners need to exercise a greater level of sensitivity and communicate the reasons for asking what might appear to be invasive questions—and they must explain the need for particular physical examinations.

The binary is so pervasive that it structures meta-discourse and narratives across various dimensions, such as identity, ideology, and politics. The binary has been effective in providing us with a mechanism by which to define, anchor, legitimate, and contextualize interpretation. Ultimately, a subject dwells within society and its culture, which provides a behavioral system with which a subject can interpret and define the world. The inventory of options contributes to identity, to what someone is or is not. Culture is the qualitative basis for the variability explaining how subjects dwell in an identity space and how judges arrive at very different interpretations of the law. Culture lays the foundation for action, conduct, strategies, and thought, which finds ultimate expression in policy. Culture thus consists of what Clifford Geertz (1973) dubs socially constructed "structures of meaning," which mediate the terms that subjects of a polity utilize to situate, organize, and define relationships between space, place, and identity. Social life is stories (Somers 1994, p. 614); therefore identities are not unitary or static, but are instead shaped by the narratives in which they are embedded. They are also constrained by the internal structures of language, the discursive production of selves in social interaction, and the politics of the spaces in which stories are expressed and received. Both stories and identities emerge from interaction; they shift and change according to the spaces and times in which they are embedded. Transgender narratives about gender identity are shaped by the particular characteristics of the contexts in which they present themselves. And they are not understood only as discourses, but also as corporeality and spaces that make available certain subject positions to actors. Transgendered individuals are able to construct narratives about themselves as people who have "chosen" their gender—who have transitioned or are in the process of transitioning. Story-actions, in turn, produce new narratives and hence new identities, politics, and communities. Narrative identities are never complete; they are always in the process of being formed. These public narratives transcend the individual; they are the cultural stereotypes that exist in the wider communities of interpretation through which stories circulate. The story of the ideal transsexual who always knew that they were of the other gender is a public narrative, or Western stereotype, that many transsexual people draw on to explain their identity to themselves and to others.

This interpretation continues to position the body as incorrect. It gives primacy to the inner "truth" of identity, thereby upholding the dichotomy between an inner truth and a wrong body. Doctors thereby created a dominant narrative of transsexual subjectivity where there was originally no coherent universal account. Patients' repetition of "proper" symptoms so as to appear intelligible to doctors, and the doctors' use of this framework to gauge intelligibility, created a narrative neither entirely accurate nor truthful. Nevertheless, this cycle installed the specific "wrong body" origin story as the standard of transsexual experience and medical diagnostics. The "born in the wrong body," or "trapped in the wrong body," narrative refers to the misalignment that individuals feel between their body and their gender identity. Although there are many trans people for whom the "wrong body" origin story does resonate, it is by no means the only way in which transgender individuals experience and narrate their bodies. The dominant narrative of the "wrong body" coincides with decades of medicalized and pathologized diagnostic criteria. The body of a trans person exists as a different entity entirely, constantly opposing an individual's true sense of self.

The establishment of the dominant origin narrative of "trans-ness" through medicine has profoundly shaped cultural narratives of trans subjects. Because of the scarcity of representation, those trans individuals who do appear are often on unscripted news and talk shows, where they are taken to be representative of all trans individuals and their experiences. Many of these representations feature trans individuals who use the "wrong body" narrative to explain their trans-ness to audiences, meaning that those representations of trans individuals that do exist are integral in reinforcing dominant origin narratives and weaving them throughout the fabric of society. It is not only interviewers who reify the "wrong body" origin story; trans people themselves also proliferate usage of this narrative throughout autobiographies, memoirs, and fictionalized texts of trans experiences. This does not mean that these individuals did not and do not truly identify with this

80   Petr Agha

origin story—but it does demonstrate the limited options that trans people have when seeking to find the language with which to describe themselves and their experiences as an intelligible origin story.

References

DVOŘÁČKOVÁ, J. Diagnóza F 64.0: Transsexualita optikou sexuologie. *Sociální studia*, 2008(1): 55–75.
FIFKOVÁ, H. Základní etapy procesu přemeny pohlaví [The major stages of a sex change]. In H. Fifková, P. Weiss, I. Procházka, P.T. Cohen-Kettenis, F. Pfäfflin, J. Veselý, V. Weiss and L. Jarolím (eds), *Transsexualita a jiné poruchy pohlavní identity* [*Transsexuality and Other Disorders of Sexual Identity*] (pp. 77–82). Praha: Grada, 2008.
GEERTZ, C. *The Interpretation of Cultures*. New York: Basic Books, 1973.
HADERKA, J.F. O jaký právní přístup k otázkám transsexualismu? *Právník*, 1986, 125(3): 213–228.
HYNIE, J. *Základy sexuologie*. Praha: Univerzita Karlova, 1974.
JAHODOVÁ, D. Konceptualizace transsexuality v českém medicínském diskurzu a dokumentárním filmu po roce 1989. *Dějiny – Teorie – Kritika: Studie a eseje*, 2011, 8(2): 289–308.
MINISTRY OF HEALTH OF THE CZECH REPUBLIC. *Communication No. LP-267-16.9.1970*, September 1970.
MINISTRY OF HEALTH OF THE CZECH REPUBLIC. *Internal Instruction No. 114-270-27.12.1979*, December 1979.
RABOCH, J. *Lékařská sexuologie*. Praha: SPN, 1984.
RAICHLOVÁ, V., and PROCHÁZKA, I. Právní aspekty [Legal aspects]. In H. Fifková, P. Weiss, I. Procházka, L. Jarolím, J. Veselý and V. Weiss (eds), *Transsexualita. Diagnostika a léčba.* [*Transsexuality: Diagnosis and Treatment*] (pp. 141–149). Praha: Grada, 2002.
SOMERS, M.R. The narrative constitution of identity: a relational and network approach. *Theory and Society*, 1994, 23(5): 605–649.
WEISS, P., FIFKOVÁ, H., and PROCHÁZKA, I. Diagnostika transsexuality. In H. Fifková, P. Weiss, I. Procházka, P.T. Cohen-Kettenis, F. Pfäfflin, J. Veselý, V. Weiss and L. Jarolím (eds), *Transsexualita a jiné poruchy pohlavní identity* (pp. 31–41). Praha: Grada, 2008.
WORKING GROUP FOR THE ISSUES OF SEXUAL MINORITIES. *Analysis of the Situation of Lesbian, Gay, Bisexual and Transgender Minority in the Czech Republic*, October 2007, online at www.vlada.cz/assets/ppov/rlp/vybory/sexualni-mensiny/EN_analyza_web.pdf

6 How the inheritance system thinks

Queering kinship, gender and care in the legal sphere

Antu Sorainen

The partial victory on equal marriage in Europe is not the end of line; other law reforms driven by equality call for fresh lines of inquiry. For this purpose, this chapter explores how alternative kinship, non-normative sexualities and gender cut through the inheritance system. In doing so, it draws on queer and feminist anthropologist literature on institutions, legal categories and relationships. It points out the vulnerability risks that gender produces in relation to the growing importance of the inheritance institution – in particular, the potentially problematic engagements with this institution by those who find themselves in the sexually marginalised groups or on the margins of kinship. The chosen case study is Finland, because its inheritance legislation is presented and conceptualised as gender-neutral and, as such, equal and just. A study of a declining Nordic welfare state provides a concrete scene from which to open up wider questions on how gender, queer sexuality and kinship interact with legal institutions. The discussion is based on original survey and interview research data on queer inheritance arrangements and lawyers' experiments with their queer clients. It analyses how gender distinctions and sexual valorisations get mobilised in and through the inheritance system.

Why the inheritance institution matters

In the situation in which most liberal European countries have equalised marriage, adoption or extended maternity rights for same-sex couples and gender discrimination clauses have been put in force, there are still always tensions between categories and institutions, the normativity of the law and human agency, and the gender binary and institutions. These legal moves impact on European cultural understandings of and social attitudes towards what sexual identities mean in society. They also mobilise kinship in novel ways, which, in turn, are directly related to the inheritance system, often in an unpredictable manner. Thus the landscape of contemporary kinship relations is rapidly changing. In this process, law is a crucial locus where categorical and interpersonal relations confront each other.

These legal and social changes in Europe took place at the outset of the European Union in the mid-1990s and escalated during the first decades of the 21st century. "Equality" was paraded in the winning of gay marriage and other legal rights for different Rainbow family and reproduction issues in most – although not all – European countries. Because most resources went into this campaigning, there has not been enough time or scholarly effort focused on new theories grounded in empirical research on what are the new exclusions and who gets marginalised after legal equality. Since "legal equality", there have been unforeseen developments, new challenges and consequences, and fields of law that have not been studied either at all or to sufficient extent from these perspectives to better understand how the gender binary works through both old and reformed legal institutions (Leckey, 2015). For example, we know virtually nothing about what happens to the posthumous wealth of lesbian, gay and other queer people in the European Union. My study of who actually inherits from queers, how they arrange their inheritance issues and what are the lawyers' attitudes to their queer clients is therefore extremely urgent.[1] Legal equality generates the old problem in new ways: "What should be done with everyone else – how should they be counted?" (Strathern, 2005, p. 157). Property offers one solution to this dilemma, because, from the point of view of the logic of the inheritance institution, the *passing* of property creates one legal arena within which to view the person, the others and their proper relations in society. In this way, the Euro-American view on kinship (Schneider, 1968), and the legal act of will-writing create the world as object and view the self as an autonomous subject.

However, the largely (hetero)normative valorisation of sexualities, as well as gender in society affects the inheritance institution and the autonomy of the individual with her/his last wishes in multiple ways. These processes take place in the complex framework combining juridical and familial values, as well as in rooted assumptions and the legal categorisations of kinship and relatedness, which all have served, in different ways, to inform the gendered inequality in the West. For example, in the United Kingdom, a 1979 study found that not only the sources of women's property are their husbands and fathers, and that only a very small minority (no more

---

1 The chapter is based on 40 interviews (conducted by the author in 2014–18) on will writing and inheritance issues with people who identify as belonging to sexually marginalised groups and two large, international online surveys on queer inheritance issues (Sorainen and Heinonen, 2016, 2017).

than 5 per cent) of women accumulated their own wealth through what is generally regarded as entrepreneurship, but also that around 60 per cent of children of rich fathers married into other wealthy families, and that testamentary freedom does not mean that people will deviate from the cultural expectations from the "natural" heirs and blood-related kinship (Harbury and Hitchens, 1979, p. 96; Finch et al, 1996).

The history of inheritance, from the Romans via the canon law to the present day has encouraged gender hierarchies, with often primogeniture (even if it had a little appeal to the Greeks) or other legal principles or social attitudes that benefited sons over daughters or surviving wives having had an imprint on the inheritance system (Accettura, 2011, pp. 230–238). It is only the late 19th and 20th centuries that developments of such principles as *coverture* – a legal doctrine whereby, upon marriage, a woman's legal rights and obligations were subsumed by those of her husband (substantially modified in 1870 in the United Kingdom, but surviving in some form until the 1960s in the United States) – or the first son's bigger share (for example in Finland since 1951) were overruled to promote a more equal stance towards gender in inheritance. This development has been partly related to urbanisation and partly to the actions of the Women's Movement alongside the growing legal rights of women.

At first, it might sound rather outdated to refer to a 1970s study and other "ancient" history. However, it is not ungrounded. A more recent study on Finland (Seppänen, 2014) shows that this trend – that is, the "right" marriage choice and family background (a good surname and certain privileged education) – have again come to determine individual positions and opportunities in society, with the super-rich getting richer and the middle classes struggling with sharply increasing housing costs, inheritance taxes and the costs of higher education, which still does not open an automatic road into the global job market. Also, in Sweden, analyses of surname distributions shows that the elite of the 18th century is still very much an elite of today: generalised and long-term social mobility in Sweden in recent years is indeed much lower than the rates reported in standard two-generation studies of the intergenerational correlation of income or education (Clark, 2013). Piketty (2013, p. 22) has convincingly demonstrated, by relying on big data, that inherited wealth now comes close to being as decisive factor in inequalities of wealth as it was in the age of Balzac, in terms of the super-wealthy families. His theory is complex, suggesting that it is essential to identify efficient redistribution wherever it exists, while also pointing out that it is "pointless to denounce every inequality as a sign of gross inefficiency that the right policy can eliminate" (Piketty, 2015, p. 121).

Leaving aside the rather troubling question of "rightness" of this or that policy, or the valorisation of inequalities in terms of "efficiency", the more pressing task here is to shed light on what role gender plays in the European inheritance system. The focus, to provide some insights into this, is on those sexually marginalised individuals who do not belong to the small elite club of the super-rich who have tended to get richer since finance capitalism and, relatedly, stock markets got a proper hold of the European countries in the 1980s. The general liberalising of wealth made it possible to speculate on import money across the national borders and laws, as a novel wave of financial deregulation and a massive faith in "self-regulating markets" escalated (Piketty, 2017, p. 2; Seppänen, 2014, p. 20). By the 2000s, the values of the stock market and estates in Europe matched those of the United States, and leading to extremely high wealth-to-income ratios in many European nation states. In France, for example, one needs to go "back to the Belle Époque era of 1900–1910 to find French wealth holders so prosperous than they have been since 2010s forward" (Piketty, 2017, p. 3). Also, in Finland, the biggest wealth holders have more than tripled their wealth during the last decade or so: in 2005, the net worth of Finland's richest person, Antti Herlin (mogul and chairman of Kone Corporation), was about €390 million; in 2014, it was already €3,000 million; in 2018, it was more than €3300 million (Seppänen, 2014, pp. 27–34; Forbes, 2018).

At the same time, developments on gender in Finland and other Nordic welfare countries, particularly in the job market, have been huge, with more women getting a higher education degree than in the 1960s. However, some recent common requirements, such as air travel for work might impact negatively on women more than on men, because of continuing inequalities in shared household duties and parental leave, both in practice and at the legislative level (Malmqvist, 2018). Meanwhile, the inheritance system is expanding because more people inherit now than before, while the wealth-to-income gap is increasing exponentially. These economic factors are heightened not only in such post-imperialist European countries as France or the United Kingdom, where there is a long-established tradition of centralised family wealth; increasingly, these developments – which Piketty (2017, p. 2) calls "a return to the pure capitalism" – are also affecting the Nordic welfare societies, which, although boasting a long social-democratic political history and reputation for equality, have been in rapid decline.

Why Finland matters

Finland serves as a fine example here. In Finland, welfare state care has been drastically diminished and state policies have been increasingly influenced by those advocating less extensive state regulation in the country – in particular, since it joined the European Union in the mid-1990s. Right-wing and populist parties have dominated government austerity programmes since the early 2000s and, especially since the 2010s, have contributed to the rapid escalation of the declining social welfare situation. The rhetoric of "no option other than cuts" has also won media space as those super-rich people (such as Antti Herlin) and the representatives or advocates of the government parties have bought or occupied leading positions in the biggest medias and also in national broadcasting company YLE.

Initially, the building of the nation state and national legislation in the latter part of the 19th century in Finland was largely based on interpretation of Hegel's philosophy.[2] Hegel articulated the structure of legacy, inheritance and history on the basis of the strictures of gathering. *Gathering* is an act of memory that determines a legacy as a legacy, a history as a history. Gathering determines an event, norm, idea or institution as something to be passed on for a future to come (Zambrana, 2012, p. 276). While Finland declared independency only in 1917, after having been a part of Sweden and then a Grand Duchy of Russia, the legislative work had been, in large part, already done in the 19th and early 20th centuries. For example, the first Finnish Penal Code was drafted by 1889 and enforced in 1894. However, the initial Swedish 1734 Inheritance Code was not fully reformed in Finland before 1965, even though there were some significant amendments such as the 1868 and 1932 inheritance amendments, the 1922 rules on the status of children born out of marriage and the marriage law of 1929, all of which impacted on kinship, family and gender equality in their own ways (Finlex, 2018).

Finland's welfare state era started in the late 1960s, after a rapid, government-initiated transformation of Finland from an agrarian state to a more modern and urban one, and it worked rather efficiently until the first decade of the 21st century.

During the peak period of the welfare system, from the late 1970s to the late 1990s, women and men in Finland could enter the job market and higher

---

2 Johan Wilhelm Snellman (1806–81) was the most influential statesman, philosopher and journalist in Finland in the 19th century. His interpretation of Hegelian philosophy formed a basis for the Finnish national movement (Fennomanics), which helped to transform Finland from a country ruled by a Swedish-speaking upper class into a country in which the Finnish-speaking majority gained cultural and political rights in the latter half of the 19th century. According to Snellman, for example, historical reading in the family deepens and widens the circle of knowledge of the entire nation (Mäkinen, 1992, pp. 10–14). In this sense, historical reading in the family sphere becomes a sort of gathering, a legacy or an inheritance for the nation to reach rationally the workings of *Geist*, the Spirit. According to Hegel (1997 [1837]), *Geist* realises itself by externalising itself in being, nature and history. Thus history is the progressive realisation of freedom through the demise of the finite. The glories and misfortunes of individuals acting in history express the realisation of the freedom of *Geist* (Zambrana, 2012, p. 275).

education without specific class or family background requirements, because the elementary public school system, the universal right to day care, state-organised elderly care, public health care, the social insurance system, progressive income taxation, and the free-of-charge, entry-by-exam-based and regionally extensive university system with state-secured low-rate student loans provided a democratic site for all young people to gain social status via knowledge gathering (Sorainen, 2015a). In other words, individuals from all walks of life could enter the system with reasonable expectations of upward mobility, regardless of gender, family background or inheritance expectations. The current developments towards privately funded higher education and private safety webs mean, however, that Finnish citizens now need to rely increasingly on their private insurances (such as private child medical insurance or private pension savings), personal support networks (family and/or relatives and friends) and care arrangements (private care homes and health care).

Thus, the significance and meanings given to kinship in everyday life, law and policymaking come to matter more than before when a welfare system is being destroyed to an increasing degree by right-wing governments. Kinship and domestic domains are increasingly affected by such new economic trends that also cross national borders. The inheritance institution inevitably influences all modern societies more than before, as Piketty (2013) has shown. What is more, even though some specific taxes, such as inheritance tax or wealth tax may be reformed at the nation state level or harmonised at the EU level, it is unlikely that the inheritance system itself will be replaced with some other redistribution system – at least, not under the current political climate, because the inheritance system effectively feeds on social inequality, on demand among those interested parties benefiting from finance capitalism (Seppänen, 2014).

These global and national trends are affecting the grass-roots level of kinship most heavily outside the new privileged "testocracy" – that is, those upper middle class and upper class students who are more likely to be admitted to elite schools because they are more likely to do well on the college tests than students coming from the lower income families (Guinier, 2015). The appearance of this new global incipient group of very well-off young people, educated in certain elite schools (most of the students admitted to competitive colleges are not poor or working class) is in demand among, and partly created by, transnational businesses. This novel group might even be named the "heritocracy", in opposition to the meritocracy, in which success was assumed to depend on one's individual competitive skills and assets.

Along the way, the national resources and wealth of the North European welfare states such as Finland have been largely transferred to tax havens, or privatised and transferred to the new business elite's enormous fees and bonus-based salaries.

Such "after-equality" (Leckey, 2015) European societies as Finland, with its short history of national wealth, and small resources (no oil, for example) are arguably influenced rather directly and severely by the inheritance wealth redistribution that is stagnating in the face of the escalating finance capitalism. Some other contemporary European societies, such as post-socialist Poland or Hungary, have had other accurate problems to solve – that is, the refugee crisis and the rise of the religious or autocratic leaders – and might not relate in the same way to the after-equality debate or the rise of the heritocracy.

In this situation, "equality" indeed seems the most promising for those members of the heritocracy who can still count on private resources, good jobs, family allowances or inheritance. In the process, not only gender and sexuality, but also kinship become crucial aspects in how the increasingly privatised care gets organised and who has access to the heritocracy. This is where the marginalised care networks the "chosen" families and novel forms of kin relations and practices come to matter in old and new ways (Mizielinska, Abramovicz and Stasinska, 2015).

Why kinship matters

My usage of the term "kinship" is open-ended, recognising the contingency of its reference field. While I take note of Sahlins' (2013, p. 25) warning not to confuse kinship and personhood relations, my approach here comes closer to Butler's (2000, p. 72) observation that the critique of the structuralist approach to kinship does not mark the end of kinship itself:

> Kinship signifies any number of social arrangements that organize the reproduction of material life, that can include the ritualization of birth and death, that provide bonds of intimate alliance both enduring and breakable, and that regulate sexuality through sanction and taboo.

As noted earlier, there are now more sexual rights and legal attention directed to gender and the situation of sexually marginalised groups in most European countries than before the era of European Union (Strathern, 2005; Harding, 2011; Leckey, 2015; Peel and Harding, 2016). However, the normative understanding of kinship as based on (heterosexual) marriage and biological children ("bio-children") produced within that marriage still dominates the debates on care rights and duties, family ties, reproduction and the status of divergent non-normative relationships. Hence many conventional legal norms still shape the significance, scope, articulations, practices and (re)imaginations of care relations among sexually marginalised people.

This happens by rerouting such practices as alternative parenting through the frameworks of legislation, economics, party politics, and the rooted valorisation of sexualities and gender roles. Norms relating to different kinship forms and care relations entail inequalities in both public and private domains, because marginalised livelihoods and significant relationships could take an endless range of shapes. As noted earlier, these often invisible, illegitimate or unrecognised care relations are directly or indirectly affected by state policies and wider economic trends, not only in how they are silenced or marginalised, but also, importantly, in terms of how they manage to survive, resist, reimagine and redescribe norms and state powers. If critical research in the socio-legal, queer and gender studies fields could make some of these particular forms thinkable and talkable, they would become "thinkable through being talkable" (Cooper, 2018). This would have huge relevance for the inheritance institution, which distributes not only wealth but also the feeling of relatedness, mainly in small heterosexual family circles (Kangas, 1996). Strathern (1981) highlighted the impact of inheritance on kin relations in her study on English kinship. According to her, the extent of "proper family feelings" is likely to be evaluated and very significant where sums of money are being passed down (Strathern, 1981, p. 104). Even though Strathern touched on the issue only briefly, her notion is highly inspiring in providing a base for further analysis of the topic. In the current Europe, the inheritance institution clearly increases economic injustice not only in society, as Piketty (2013) has shown, but also in the family, as the recent survey results on sexually marginalised groups in six European countries indicates (Sorainen, 2018a).

Strathern (2005, p. viii) also pointed out that there is a particular purchase to introducing legal thinking into the study of kinship, since, as a discipline and practice, the law has to deal with different kinds of relationships. The law is the classic locus for situations in which categorical and interpersonal relations confront each other. The law explicitly and centrally deals with persons in relation to categories. Importantly, American anthropologist Kath Weston (1991) has questioned the exclusions and inclusions of the kinship terminology because queer people who often live in nonconforming relations tended to became *exiles from kinship* – on the levels of both the state and the biological family. This might impact the inheritance arrangements in families in unfair ways, more often than expected by any assumedly "gender-neutral" law: queer daughters might be pushed into care duties, while gay sons may be silently made to give up their inheritance shares or to testament their own estate to blood relatives instead of to their partners or support community because they often internalised a certain guilty feeling, the "not deserving" role in the heterosexual family order (Sorainen, 2018b). Here, again, Strathern (2005) is helpful, underlining that certain "facts" of kinship are a matter not only of the law, but also of rooted cultural assumptions.

If we think of an efficient tool, or a device, for the analysis of the impact of the inheritance institution on gender and non-heteronormative sexualities, I believe that the realities of marginalised care relations are best analysed by contrasting divergent margins of *kinship* rather than families, chosen or not. In this way, we will gain more nuanced and sophisticated knowledge and data on what different margins and marginalisations are about in terms of gender and sexuality – what are the margins of margins and what kind of hierarchies are mobilised inside of margins. For example, the question of the intersectionalities of marginalised genders and sexualities versus other factors such as age, class, and legal realities may cut through the inheritance system in surprisingly different, but also similar ways in different countries.

Why institutions and legal categories matter

Kinship is something that we all are supposed have, because we all were born with some relation – be that relation the person from whose womb we emerged, or someone who owned or declared us as their child when we were new-born, or someone who acted as our legal guardian. For the EU citizens and the citizens of other European nation states, at the lowest level the primary relationship as a citizen would be with the state, in the event that one gets abandoned, as a new-born, with unidentified parents.[3] All European citizens have a surname and some kind of an identity proof, which makes them individuals – "persons" contrasted with "dividuals" (Smith, 2012), or with being a representative of a clan, tribe or household – who might claim and practise their right to express their assumedly personal, authentic and autonomous will in the legal context – ultimately, by writing a will (Sorainen, 2018c; Strathern, 1992, pp. 21–23). The state interferes in this specific right only if it recognises legal heirs that are not taken into proper consideration according to its institutional inheritance logic. For example, in Finland, the legal logic of inheritance constitutes of a "legal share", which means that all legal children, regardless of their gender or the closeness of their relationship with the testator, are entitled to an equal share of the estate. In the event that there are no such children, the hierarchical logic of kinship and then relationality will be applied, and

---

3 Institutionalised child abandonment has, at times, been truly a mass phenomenon in modern Europe. In these systems, the identity of the mother was left unknown, and the state institutions assumed the role of the parent and the guardian of the child (Tapaninen, 2004, p. 1).

inheritance taxation increases gradually where the relationship is thought to be more distanced from the core logic, with the final heir, in the absence of others being the state.

But what constitutes an "institution"? Minimally, an institution is only a convention, argues Mary Douglas (1986, p. 46): conventions arise when all parties have a common interest in there being a rule to insure coordination, on which no one has a conflicting interest and from which none will deviate lest the common interest is lost. A convention, to that extent, is thus "self-policing". The inheritance system, as an institution, could thus be seen as the minimal convention of what forms kinship in a certain (legal) culture. Further, inheritance laws define the minimal convention of what forms those kin relations that count in a certain state.

As noted, the inheritance institution, which is always inherently about legal categories of relatedness, valorises the financial weight of kin positions as it defines the "inheritance family" (Monk, 2014). In Finland, for example, aunts and uncles belong to this institutional "family", which is entitled (following certain hierarchical kinship order) to inheritance, while cousins are excluded. In some other legislative cultures, such as Russia, the inheritance family is formed according to a rather similar (Euro-American) understanding of marriage and legal "children" than in the EU sphere. However, the Russian inheritance institution's logic considerably extends the boundaries of the inheritance family unit, and also imposes more obligations on the testator and the members of the inheritance family. Hence, where the Russian law limits testamentary freedom and inheritance rights by requiring certain care relations from the potential heirs, Finnish law looks at a certain kin relation status as the only relation that really matters, in terms of one's eligibility as a proper "heir". In other words, in Russia, more than in Finland, the person as an individual turns out to be the person as a relative, in an actual relationship; hence the inheritance family may create a different family from a "genetic family" – in particular, if the legal heir will be the state (Strathern, 2005, pp. 10–20).

In addition to promoting and defining who counts as a relative and what are the limits for the de-kinning one's blood line or adding non-blood people to one's kin through one's will, inheritance laws often also place financial value tags on different sorts of relationships. In Finland, the married spouse, regardless of sex (different or same) pays significantly less inheritance tax than a cohabitee. Accordingly, one's legal child pays significantly less inheritance tax than one's social child, however close or real the parenting situation. In this way, the current Finnish inheritance taxation system positions siblings raised in Rainbow families unequally in inheritance situations. The children in the same Rainbow family might be due to pay hugely different sums of inheritance tax because the family unit may consist of more than two parents, of whom some might not be legally defined as part of the same inheritance family (donors and co-parents). This forced economic valuation of actual family relations arguably pushes Rainbow family parents towards the conventional forms of marriage and couplehood (Sorainen, 2016).

But how do these factors and tensions between legal fictions and rooted cultural assumptions and social practices get actualised in the real-life inheritance arrangements of different sexually marginalised groups?

How the institution thinks and how individuals act

According to an online survey among lawyers (Sorainen and Heinonen, 2017[4]), the inheritance institution's heteronormative logic is not often contested or scrutinised by lawyers' queer clients. For example, those members of Finnish Rainbow families who are in the most unjust situations do not look for legal advice to the extent that one might expect (see Figure 6.1).

Finnish lawyers meet queer clients mostly in divorce and separation situations. Further, Finnish queer people do not often seek to engage in inheritance tax planning or to write their will (see Figure 6.2).

One (speculative) explanation for the small portion of the parent-identified non-legal Rainbow mothers and fathers who look for legal advice in Finland could be that inheritance questions have not been brought up in the public debate, which has been largely dominated by questions about the equal marriage, internal adoption and maternal rights for the co-mother.

10% of Rainbow bio-mothers sought legal advice

7% of parent-identified Rainbow mothers without a legal tie to the child sought legal advice

3.5% of donors and parent-identified Rainbow fathers without a legal tie to the child sought legal advice

Figure 6.1 Proportion of Rainbow families who sought legal advice in Finland, 2016.

---

4 The online survey *Lawyers on Inheritance Arrangements among Rainbow Clients* was open between 22 May and 22 June 2017, available in both English and Finnish. It aimed to find out the specific legal issues on which queer people seek advice from lawyers, and to raise consciousness among lawyers and legal experts of the importance of proper knowledge of the legal needs of the LBGTQI clients. There were 112 respondents in total: 104 from Finland; 4 from Australia; 2 from the United States; and 2 from the United Kingdom.

only

7%

have done inheritance
tax planning

Gay men and heterosexual men do tax planning
twice as frequently as lesbian or other women

Tax planning is most usually done for the
benefit of legal partners
or godchildren

Figure 6.2 Proportion of inheritance-related tax planning among the survey
respondents, 2016.

Also, as a result of rather recent changes in these laws in Finland (registered partnership for same-sex couples became possible in 2002; same-sex marriage, in 2017; internal family adoption, in 2009; external adoption, in 2017; the maternal law reform granting motherhood also to the non-biological mother, in 2018), many Rainbow parents are in their 30s and 40s, and raising underage children. Arguably, they may not yet have come "naturally" to that life phase in which one starts seriously to think about old age, death and the passing of one's estate.

In the interviews, the issue of sperm donors did not come up, but if the donor has signed in anonymity, the child will not, by law, inherit from him unless he writes a will for the child's benefit. Perhaps donors do not, for the most part, look to change this situation, even if they are present in a child's life? Co-mothers and co-fathers without a legal tie to the child in Rainbow families are in a similar situation, and they may need to be careful to look for legal advice, because their position has been more vulnerable in the family than that of the biological mother.

Then again, one would assume that the complicated and, in terms of many queer relationships and family constellations unfair inheritance tax categorisation system that puts non-legal social children in a worse economic position than bio-children would prompt co-parents and active donors to look for inheritance planning advice in Finland. The inheritance tax bill payable by a social child could be almost three times more than that payable by a legal or bio-child, because social children and co-parents are categorised as "strangers" to each other in terms of Finnish inheritance tax law under which tax categories significantly depend not only on estate value, but also on types of (family) relationship (VERO, 2018). In the same family, one of the siblings could inherit from the bio-mother and the bio-father without paying the higher rate of tax, while other siblings may inherit only from the bio-mother and, in the event that they inherit also from the non-legal co-mother or co-father, will need to pay often more than double the "stranger" tax. The stranger inheritance tax category applies also in the event of co-habitation, or other long-term or otherwise significant relationship outside of marriage or registered partnership.

These divergent inheritance situations in terms of queer relationships and families could lead to very complex situations for some of the children in Finnish Rainbow families, or queer co-habitees, long-term lovers or partners in vulnerable inheritance situations. Here, gender arguably plays a significant part because gay men are more active than lesbian women in arranging their inheritances, as men generally write wills more often than women (Sorainen and Heinonen, 2016[5]). As Figure 6.2 shows, the huge majority (93 per cent) of queer respondents had not done any tax planning. This might be a result of the inherent homophobia presumed among queer people, leading them sometimes to think that the inheritance system does not belong to them.

The low number of Rainbow co-parents looking for legal advice in inheritance issues could thus spring from a "feeling" of dis-attachment. The continued marginalisation of sexuality and gender perspectives beyond those that are embedded in conjugal reproductive heterosexuality in the Finnish inheritance legislation may have alienated many queer people from the inheritance institution altogether. For example, those co-mothers who are divorced sometimes think that their estate belongs to their blood relatives, such as nieces and nephews, because "this is what the law says, and the law knows best" (one interviewed woman, b. 1962). It could also be, as in this specific case, that the bio-children of the divorced partner had treated the co-parent in a homophobic way, leading to a situation in which the divorced co-parent's motivation to pass her estate on to the divorced partner's bio-children is very low or non-existent. These kinds of situations

5 The online survey *Wills and Inheritance Arrangements in Sexually Marginalised Groups* was open between 18 December 2015 and 29 January 2016, and was available in six languages: English; Russian; Hungarian; Romanian; Swedish; and Finnish. It aimed to find out in which ways lesbian, gay and other sexually marginalised groups of people, as well as persons identifying as transgender could get more and better information about the ways in which they might arrange their inheritance – such as by writing a will or by other means – to benefit those people whom they choose. There were 1,007 respondents: 158 in English; 108 in Russian; 101 in Hungarian; 74 in Romanian; 56 in Swedish; and 510 in Finnish. In total, 53.4% of the respondents were from Finland. Roughly 40% of the Finnish respondents identified as lesbian, 26% as gay, 20% as queer, 24% as bisexual, 10% as poly or non-monogamous, 8% as straight, 7% as other and 2% as asexual.

might convince one about the rightness of the saying "blood is thicker than water", which in turn leads to situations in which queer relations do not translate into queer wills, as Westwood (2015) has shown.

Another reason – not totally unjustified – for the comparatively low level of queer people looking for legal advice in inheritance issues might be the mistrust to lawyers' ability to comprehend the queer specific family and relationship problems. Evidence from the interview data lends weight to this explanation, with a number of informants directly mentioning that they do not trust lawyers to understand the specificities of queer relationships. According to the open answers in the 2016 survey, a number of respondents explained how ill-informed advice from heteronormative or ignorant lawyers had made their problems worse. To contrast this, many Finnish lawyers – according to the 2017 survey – firmly believe that the existing inheritance legislation is just in terms of the diversity of gender and sexualities. Therefore they think that, as proper legal professionals, they need to stay "neutral" and not pay attention to the specificities of the queer issues when meeting queer clients.

It is interesting to contrast this gender and sex "neutral" Finnish lawyers' culture with the American, Australian and British lawyers' responses to the 2017 survey. As a rule, they described in detail why they saw it as extremely important to advise their queer clients to pay careful attention to the shortcomings and possible "traps" for queer people within the inheritance system. The tragic history of HIV and AIDS has taught the gay community, and also queer-friendly lawyers, that anti-gay relatives may well challenge those wills that are written for the benefit of the gay community and that – in particular, in the past – judges have often decided against queer wills for the benefit of blood relatives, on the basis that intestacy laws and trial judges aim to represent the "thinking of the average citizen", who is presumably heterosexual and reproduces children in marriage. U.S. intestacy laws also tend to represent the interests of government, in that they favour those who were assumed to be dependent on the testator during life (Accettura, 2011, p. 248).

For these reasons, many US and UK lawyers actively advise their queer clients to establish a trust, instead of writing a will, because it is a safer defence against a potential challenge on the part of relatives. In a similar note, one of the American lawyers answered the survey question, "If your Rainbow client does not have a strong plan already, to which directions or in which ways do you advise them, in terms of structuring their wills or other inheritance-related arrangements?" as follows:

> Everyone needs a plan in place (even if you don't have a lot of $) bc the law assumes heteronormative family structure (re inheritance,

decision-making authority). A plan should reflect only the client's wishes re inheritance, guardianship for minor children, decision-makers. I always discuss specific disinheritance or exclusion provisions for legally-related family who may cause trouble.

(Response no. 24)

At the same time, a typical Finnish lawyer's answer followed these lines:

I do not direct them in any way but ask what they want or aim to. After this, I will tell them what are the possibilities that the law offers in regards of their wishes and situation.

(Response no. 75)

Arguably, where the American lawyers took the inequality of law and inheritance institution as a given, in Finland faith in the equality and justness of the "legal share" influenced the attitudes of both the lawyers and the queer respondents: the logic of the inheritance institution was not questioned.

Ultimately, the European inheritance system reflects the ideal of the autonomy and equality of the modern individual, and provides the citizen with a right to define (within certain limits) the destiny of their *gatherings*. However, if one does not feel deserving of a full citizenship or an equal family role, as a result of the complex and long history of discrimination and non-recognition of queer people and queer lives in society, then perhaps one does not believe in one's right to exercise one's potentialities in this field fully – and hence does not question the dominantly heteronormative logic of the kinship ideology working through and with the inheritance institution.

Of the Finnish queer respondents who had been involved in inheritance dispute, only 46 per cent had used legal assistance (see Figure 6.3).

Figure 6.3 Proportion of respondents identifying as queer who had been involved in inheritance-related disputes, 2016.

In the current EU legal sphere in which (neo)liberal ideas undermining the individual choice and individual rights have been favoured more than conservative or homophobic views, sexual rights have been granted to more people and social groups. Therefore intergenerational and interpersonal queer dependencies may be judged through less heteronormative lenses by the state, the lawmakers, the trial judges and the lawyers, and perhaps even by the wider society (the relatives). Family forms, sexual choices and relationship practices, as well as the legal and social structures and realities of the society within which these occur have become more diverse in many ways in the last two decades or so, although the liberal stress on individual rights also creates new marginalisations and invisibilities (Rubin, 1984). In this process, the inheritance institution will most probably become of more relevance to more queer-headed families and queer individuals than it has been in the past. In this process, sexual hierarchies, valorisations and also gender *matters*.

Why queer(y)ing the inheritance system matters

The increasing range of new family units and care or dependency relationships that do not return to normative biological reproduction, couple form, marriage or intimacy urgently requires the redefinition and reimagination of kinship, relationships, family and other categories that address inheritance rules and taxonomies. Most lesbian and gay people do not have children, civil partners or marital spouses, although the number of children growing in complex (Rainbow) families, and the diversity of non-heterosexual intimate relations, households and parenting has become more visible in the society. According to Finnish official statistics from 2012, people older than 60 registered their same-sex partnerships less often than did younger generations, and women constituted a clear majority (60 per cent) of registered same-sex households.[6] Although this represents significant social and cultural transformation the distribution of "queer wealth" through the inheritance system is an underrepresented research topic. Therefore it is virtually

---

6 There are no exact statistics on the number of children growing in Rainbow families in the European Union. In 2016, the Union totalled 220 million households, almost a third of which (65.6 million) had dependent children. The share of "reconstituted families" in families with underage children is 9% and, on average, reconstituted families have slightly more children than families with children in general. The mother brought 59% of the children into the family. In Finland, there were 2,700 families of registered same-sex couples in 2016, while in 669 families with children, the parents were a registered same-sex couple. The number of Rainbow families with children almost doubled in the span of five years, but it is impossible to get exact numbers because Rainbow families are so complex that statistical categories do not reach the reality (Eurostat, 2018; Statistics Finland, 2013, 2016).

unknown what happens to the posthumous wealth of those lesbian, gay and other non-heteronormative European people who get older and die without children, or are not in a civil partnership or marriage.[7]

What creates a relation

In the Finnish inheritance law system, the "forced heirship" principle leaves, at maximum, only 50 per cent freedom for the testator's own choice of how to distribute their estate in the event that there are legal heirs. In cases in which there are no sufficiently legally close relatives (which category includes children and grandchildren, parents and grandparents, aunts and uncles, nieces and nephews), the testator is free to write a will totally according to their own wishes. Where there is neither will nor legal heirs, the state will inherit the estate, and it needs to deal with it according to a specific set of rules.

Inheritance relations are, however, embedded in legal and economic frameworks extending beyond the nation state and its laws. In the European Union, this means that the local inheritance legislation is impacted also by EU harmonising laws and also, partly, by international agreements. Member states also look to prevent their citizens from abusing the system by relocating to other countries for tax reasons. Finland, for example, has been renegotiating its tax agreement with Portugal to prevent a group of 200–300 super-rich Finns from escaping Finnish tax regulations by moving to Portugal, where they escape inheritance and pension taxation, which loss of tax revenue for the Finnish state would be, for this one "social group" alone, a few million euros (Konttinen, 2018). To contrast this, according to my interview data and the 2016 survey, some queer people who have relocated to spend their retirement days in such warmer and cheaper countries as Spain or Thailand have had considerable problems with inheritance issues as homophobic relatives have tried to cut them off from family inheritances if they have established new queer relationships in their new location, as the relatives (or lawyers) are unwilling to recognise such cross-cultural relations as significant.

Such problems may partly be the result of the currently dominating equal marriage form, which connects all sexualities to the reproductive couple

---

7 See, however, Sorainen (2015b); Sorainen and Heinonen (2016, 2017); Mizielinska et al (2015). Recent British studies have discussed queer will-writing and aging within the legal sphere of testamentary freedom: Monk (2013, 2014); Harding (2015); Westwood (2015).

mode that gathers and distributes wealth within the core family (Duggan, 2003). For example, in 2017, Finland decided to considerably ease the inheritance tax of the biggest estates, as well as the taxation of lifetime gifts. This reform benefited mostly those citizens who earned more than €7,000 per month. With the average income in Finland in 2017 less than €3,000, it is clear that the country wanted to support its richest citizens via their kinship and marriage choices. This was clearly an anti-welfare political move that would promote social inequality and increase income and wealth gaps. It could also been seen as a move to increase the gender wealth gap, because Finnish women earn about 20 per cent less than men and have less high-ranking positions in the job market. Either way, it was thus a legislative move apt to increase inequality in society, as well as unjust relations between gender and inherited wealth.

According to the survey results (Sorainen and Heinonen, 2016), Finnish men in all sexual categories (gay, bi, straight and queer) write more wills than Finnish women in any sexual category (lesbian, bi, straight, queer) (see Figure 6.4).

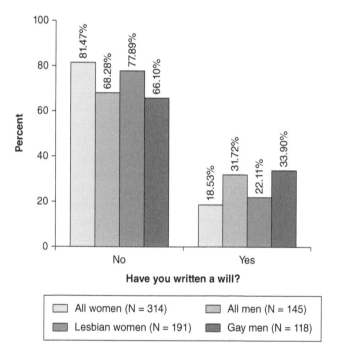

Figure 6.4 Proportion of lesbian and gay survey respondents who had written a will, compared with all women and men, 2016.

Even though lesbian women write wills more often than all women, they still do this significantly less often than all men or gay men. Also, as we saw in Figure 6.2, gay men engage in tax planning twice as often as lesbian women. All in all, will-writing and tax planning, in light of the 2016 survey results, seem to be practices that men engage more closely with than women.

Why reimagining the inheritance institution matters

In today's challenging economic and political situation in the European Union, new cross-cultural realities of privilege are creating unpredictable social margins and exclusions. The prevailing discourses of kinship, influenced by state ideologies, national legislation and legal fictions regarding the inheritance institution strongly influence individual decisions on reproduction, parenting, care, material support webs and dependency relations in the sexual and gender margins.

Accordingly, as we have seen in this chapter, the cultural valorisation of sexualities and genders influences the ways in which lesbian women and gay men engage with the inheritance institution. Unfortunately, the long history of discrimination and the normative legal categorisations of relatedness, as well as "neutral" attitudes towards queer specificities among lawyers in such European welfare countries in transition such as Finland, might create many unjust scenes. This could make queer people – in particular, queer women and many children in Rainbow families – more vulnerable in terms of "fair" inheritance wealth distribution than straight people – in particular, men. As we have seen, one clear gender-related difference regarding the inheritance institution is that gay men write wills more often than lesbian women and that men do so more often than women.

New and old laws concerning inheritance may either encourage or force individuals to design unconventional and novel forms with which to solve the way in which the inheritance institution can cut through normative assumptions on kinship and gender. For example, in Ireland, two gay men, aged 58 and 82, married in December 2017 to avoid the higher inheritance tax. The two men claimed never to have been romantically or sexually involved with each other (O'Laughlin, 2017): "He said, 'You need somewhere to live, and I need someone to take care of me'," Mr O'Sullivan recalled. "Why don't we join forces?"

Currently, there has been a conservative backlash, often supported by religious institutions or new populist parties, against so-called broken families and non-conforming sexualities. This is happening everywhere in the European Union – in the Nordic welfare state of Finland, as well as in the former socialist countries – and it is often supported by new restrictive legislations and policies (Sorainen et al, 2017). There is therefore a dire need for academic insight into the patterns of social exclusion produced by the inheritance institution because so many novel and/or unpredictable or unforeseen "afters" are appearing in the turmoil of both liberal law reforms and the rise of right-wing governmental politics across the member states. This would also help (perhaps force?) the inheritance institution to reimagine its understandings of kinship and care relations by questioning some of its implicit hierarchies and explicit categorisations, redirecting them more justly towards to redefine answers to the old question of "what kinship is all about" (Schneider, 1968).

This direction is, in my view, one of radical diversity combined with new conceptions of kinship and state. Equality, if the only leading star in politics, tends to erase diversity and creates unjust enclaves in which the experience of community or the shared experience of relatedness is no more shared.

References

Accettura, M.P. (2011) *Blood and Money: Why Families Fight over Inheritance and What to Do about It?* Farminton Hills, MI: Collingwood Press.

Butler, J. (2000) *Antigone's Claim: Kinship between Life and Death.* New York: Columbia University Press.

Clark, G. (2013) "What is the true rate of social mobility in Sweden? *A surname analysis, 1700–2012*" [online]. Available at: http://faculty.econ.ucdavis.edu/faculty/gclark/The%20Son%20Also%20Rises/Sweden%202014.pdf

Cooper, D. (2018) "Can projects of reimagining complement critical research?", *social politics and stuff,* 20 April [online]. Available at: https://davinascooper.wordpress.com/2018/04/20/can-projects-of-reimagining-complement-critical-research/

Douglas, M. (1986) *How Institutions Think.* Syracuse, NY: Syracuse University Press.

Duggan, L. (2003) *The Twilight of Equality? Neoliberalism, Cultural Politics, and the Attack on Democracy.* Boston, MA: Beacon Press.

Eurostat (2018) "Families with children in the EU" [online]. Available at: http://ec.europa.eu/eurostat/web/products-eurostat-news/-/EDN-20170531-1?inheritRedirect=true

Finch, J., Hayes, L. Mason, J., and Wallis, L. (1996) *Wills, Inheritance and Families.* London: Polity Press.

Finlex (2018) "Finlex data bank", *Ministry of Justice in Finland* [online]. Available at: www.finlex.fi/en/

Forbes (2018) "Profile/Antti Herlin" [online]. Available at: www.forbes.com/profile/antti-herlin/

Guinier, L. (2015) *The Tyranny of the Meritocracy: Democratizing Higher Education in America.* Boston, MA: Beacon Press.

Harbury, C.D., and Hitchens, D.M.W.N. (1979) *Inheritance and Wealth Inequality in Britain*. London and Boston, MA: Allen & Unwin.

Harding, R. (2011) *Regulating Sexuality. Legal Consciousness in Lesbian and Gay Lives*. Abingdon and New York: Routledge.

Harding, R. (2015) "The rise of statutory wills and the limits of best interests decision-making in inheritance", *Modern Law Review*, 78(6), pp. 945–970.

Hegel, G.W.F. (1997 [1837]) *Reason in History: A General Introduction to the Philosophy of History*. Trans. R.S. Hartman. Upper Saddle River, NJ: Prentice Hall.

Kangas, U. (1996) *Perinnöt ja testamentit [Legacies and Wills]*. Helsinki: Yliopistopaino.

Konttinen, M. (2018) "Hallituksen mitta täyttyi: Haluaa irtisanoa Suomen ja Portugalin välisen verosopimuksen – varakkaiden suomalaiseläkeläisten verovapaus päättyy [Government measure met: it wants to terminate the tax agreement between Finland and Portugal – the tax exemption of wealthy Finnish pensioners ends]", *YLE*, 12 April [online]. Available at: https://yle.fi/uutiset/3-10156694

Leckey, R. (ed.) (2015) *After Legal Equality: Family, Sex, Kinship*. New York: Routledge.

Mäkinen, I. (1992) "Snellman kansankirjastoista ja lukemisesta [Snellman on public libraries and reading]". *Kirjastotiede ja informatiikka*, 11(1), pp. 10–24.

Malmqvist, A. (2018) "Swedish lesbian mothers arrange parental leave: the heteronormative, homonormative and non-normative ways", in U. Dahl, J. Mizielinska, A. Sorainen and R. Uibo (eds), *Queer(y)ing Kinship in the Baltic Region and Beyond: The Geopolitics of LGBTQ Reproduction, Family and Intimate Life*. Stockholm: Södertörn Academic Press, forthcoming.

Mizielinska, J., Abramovicz, M., and Stasinska, A. (2015) *Families of Choice in Poland: Family Life of Non-Heterosexual People*. Warsaw: Instytut Psychologii Polskiej Akademii Nauk.

Monk, D. (2013) "EM Forster's will: an overlooked posthumous publication", *Legal Studies*, 33(4), pp. 572–597.

Monk, D. (2014) "Sexuality and children post-equality", in R. Leckey (ed.), *After Legal Equality: Family, Sex, Kinship*. New York: Routledge, pp. 200–215.

O'Laughlin, E. (2017) "In Ireland, a same-sex marriage with a tax benefit", *New York Times*, 24 December [online]. Available at: www.nytimes.com/2017/12/24/world/europe/ireland-gay-marriage-inheritance-tax.html

Peel, E., and Harding, R. (eds) (2016) *Ageing and Sexualities: Interdisciplinary Perspectives*. Farnham: Ashgate.

Piketty, T. (2013) *Capital in the Twenty-First Century*. Cambridge, MA, and London: Belknap/Harvard University Press.

Piketty, T. (2015) *The Economics of Inequality*. Cambridge, MA, and London: Belknap/Harvard University Press.

Piketty, T. (2017) *Chronicles on Our Troubled Times*. London: Penguin Books.

Rubin, G. (1984) "Thinking sex: notes for a radical theory of the politics of sexuality", in C.S. Vance (ed.), *Pleasure and Danger: Exploring Female Sexuality*. Boston, MA: Routledge and Kegan Paul, pp. 267–319.

Sahlins, M. (2013) *What Kinship Is – And Is Not*. Chicago, IL, and London: University of Chicago Press.

Schneider, D.M. (1968) *American Kinship: A Cultural Account* (Anthropology of Modern Societies Series). Englewood Cliffs, NJ: Prentice-Hall.

Seppänen, E. (2014) *Suomen rikkaat: kuka kukin on* [*The Rich in Finland: Who is Who*]. Helsinki: Minerva.

Smith, K. (2012) "From dividual and individual selves to porous subjects", *The Australian Journal of Anthropology*, 23, pp. 50–64.

Sorainen, A. (2015a) "We are not containers! On experimental objects, past struggles and alternatives for education", *AllegraLab* [online]. Available at: http://allegralaboratory.net/we-are-not-containers-on-experimental-objects-past-struggles-and-alternatives-for-education/

Sorainen, A. (2015b) "Queer personal lives, inheritance perspectives, and small places", *Nordic Journal for Queer Studies: Lambda Nordica*, 19(3–4), pp. 31–54.

Sorainen, A. (2016) "Inheritance system and care: queer will-writing" [online]. Available at: http://revaluingcare.net/inheritance-system-and-care-queer-will-writing/

Sorainen, A. (2018a) "Lesbian inheritance arrangements", *Journal of Lesbian Studies*, forthcoming.

Sorainen, A. (2018b) "Gay back alley Tolstoys and inheritance perspectives: re-imagining kinship in queer margins", in P. Boyce, S. Posecco and E.J. Gletz (eds), *Queering Knowledge: Analytics, Devices and Investments after Marilyn Strathern*. London: Routledge, forthcoming.

Sorainen, A. (2018c) "Kinship in Europe", in *LGBTQI: Encyclopedia of Transnational Gender and Sexualities*. Farmington Hills, MI: Schribner, forthcoming.

Sorainen, A., and Heinonen, A. (2016) *Wills and Inheritance in Sexually Marginalised Groups, Online survey 18.12. 2015–29.1. 2016*. University of Helsinki: Department of Philosophy, History, Culture and Arts [online]. Available at: http://antusorainen.com/main-survey-results/

Sorainen, A., and Heinonen, A. (2017) *Lawyers' Attitudes on Inheritance Arrangements among Their Rainbow Clients, Online survey 22.5. 2017–22.6. 2017*. University of Helsinki: Department of Philosophy, History, Culture and Arts [online]. Available at: http://antusorainen.com/main-survey-results/

Sorainen, A., Avdeeva, A., Zhabenko, A., and Isupova, O. (2017) "Strategies of non-normative families, parenting and reproduction in neo-traditional Russia: An Open Space Roundtable", *Families, Relationships and Societies*, 6(3), pp. 471–486.

Statistics Finland (2013) "Families" [online]. Available at: www.stat.fi/artikkelit/2013/art_2013-09-23_001.html

Statistics Finland (2016) "Families" [online]. Available at: www.stat.fi/til/perh/2016/perh_2016_2017-05-26_tie_001_en.html

Statistics Finland (2018) "Economy and livelihood" [online]. Available at: www.stat.fi/tup/tasaarvo/economy-and-livelihood/index_en.html#_ga=2.251263878.1879531200.1524739904-2075809190.1524739904

Strathern, M. (1981) *Kinship at the Core: Anthropology of Elmdon, a Village in North-West Essex in the Nineteenth-Sixties*. London and New York: Cambridge University Press.

Strathern, M. (1992) *Reproducing the Future: Anthropology, Kinship and the New Reproductive Technologies*. Manchester: Routledge.

Strathern, M. (2005) *Kinship, Law and the Unexpected: Relatives Are Always a Surprise*. London and New York: Cambridge University Press.

Tapaninen, A. (2004) "Motherhood through the wheel: the care of foundlings in late c19th Naples", in P. Willson (ed.), *Gender, Family and Sexuality: The Private Sphere in Italy 1860–1945*. Basingstoke: Palgrave Macmillan, pp. 50–70.

VERO (2018) "Individuals/inheritance" [online]. Available at: www.vero.fi/en/individuals/property/inheritance/

Weston, K. (1990) *Families We Choose: Lesbians, Gays, Kinship*. New York: Columbia University Press.

Westwood, S. (2015) "Complicating kinship and inheritance: older lesbians' and gay men's will-writing in England", *Feminist Legal Studies*, 23(2), pp. 181–197.

Zambrana, R. (2012) "Hegel's legacy", *The Southern Journal of Philosophy*, 50(2), pp. 273–284.

Index